CHAMELEON
PRESS

The Kiplings returning to England from the Cape in 1907 on the *Kenilworth Castle*. Kipling with characteristic cap and pipe stands behind his wife Carrie (in fur coat); behind him is the young architect, Herbert Baker, who designed the Kiplings' Cape Town home. Elsie and John Kipling are seated, in visible discomfort, on deck.

Reneé Durbach

KIPLING'S
SOUTH AFRICA

To the home of the floods and thunder,
To her pale dry healing blue –
To the lift of the great Cape combers,
And the smell of the baked Karroo.
To the growl of the sluicing stamp-head –
To the reef and the water-gold,
To the last and the largest Empire,
To the map that is half unrolled!

("The Native-Born", 1894)

Chameleon Press

Cover illustration (from the Kipling Collection,
University of Cape Town Libraries):

This anti-war cartoon from the 1900 Christmas issue of the British magazine *Truth* is entitled "Paardeberg 1907" and brings together, in a prophecy of reconciliation, all the major figures of the Anglo-Boer War. Kruger and Lord Roberts – "not enemies but close allies", and united in a "motor-chariot" that flies the British flag – are passing judgement on the bare-headed prisoner Rhodes, whose "dreams of Empire" have cost both sides so dearly "in life and limb and land". In the background, Boer and Tommy stand side by side, while at the forefront Kipling writes a new poem – called "The Present Minded Burgher" in contrast to those pro-war verses on "The Absent-Minded Beggar" which had proved so popular.

CHAMELEON PRESS

First edition 1988
Published by Chameleon Press
19 Estmil Road, Diep River 7800
(Postal address: PO Box 117, Plumstead 7800)

Designed by Linda Vicquery
Captions and introduction: Lynne Bryer
Setting & Reproduction: ProSet-Flexoplate
Printed and bound by CTP Book Printers

ISBN 0 620 12477 6

Contents

Acknowledgements, 6
Introduction, 7

In the hands of Fate, 9
The life unaltered, 21
Gentlemen in khaki, 29
Lessons of the war, 49
The deeper peace, 61
Half the horizon, 82
A dreams ends, 97

Notes, 103
Map of Cape Peninsula, 104
Picture credits, 105
Chronology, 106
Select bibliography, 110
Index, 111

Acknowledgements

I am greatly appreciative of the help and enthusiasm of the following people of the University of Cape Town libraries: Sue Gorton, custodian of the Kipling Collection, and Celia Walters and their colleagues in the African Studies Library, Leonie Twentyman Jones and Etaine Eberhard of the Archives and Manuscripts department, and William Pelston of the photographic department.

My gratitude, too, to Information Department Head Arlene Fanarof and her colleagues and researcher Jenny Walters at the South African Library, and Maryke Jooste of the Library of Parliament.

In addition, my thanks to the following people and organisations throughout South Africa: Africana Museum, Johannesburg; Mrs Margaret Cairns, Cape Town; The Campbell Collection of the University of Natal, Durban; The Cape Archives Depot, Cape Town; Cory Library for Historical Research, Rhodes University Library, Grahamstown; Mrs Lavinia de Klerk, Cape Town; East London Museum; Free State Archives Depot, Bloemfontein; Immelman Collection, University of Cape Town Libraries; Johannesburg Art Gallery; Killie Campbell Africana Library, Durban; Kimberley Public Library; McGregor Museum, Kimberley; Dr Frank Mitchell, Cape Town; The Municipal Reference Library, Cape Town; National English Literary Museum, Grahamstown; Dr Cecily Niven, Amanzi, Uitenhage; Mr Francois Petousis, Cape Town; Mrs Wendy Pickstone, Lekkerwijn, Groot Drakenstein; Mr Michael Pickstone-Taylor, Lekkerwijn, Groot Drakenstein; The Olive Schreiner Collection, University of Cape Town Libraries; The Cecil J Sibbett Collection, University of Cape Town Libraries; Simon's Town Museum; Transvaal Archives Depot, Pretoria; War Museum of the Boer Republics, Bloemfontein; University of the Witwatersrand, Johannesburg.

I would also like to thank the following sources in Britain: Bank of England, London; John Beal & Son, Brighton; The Kipling Society, London; The Mansell Collection Limited, London; The National Trust, London; Rhodes House Library, Oxford; University of Sussex Library, Brighton; A P Watt, London.

Finally, I would like to thank: the Alexander Turnbull Library, Wellington, New Zealand; Auckland Public Library, Auckland, New Zealand; Dalhousie University Library, Halifax, Nova Scotia, Canada; The Houghton Library, Harvard University, Cambridge, Massachusetts, USA; Ladies' Home Journal, New York, USA; The Library, Princeton University, New Jersey, USA; Yale University Library, Connecticut, USA; National Archives of Zimbabwe, Harare.

While notes have been kept to a minimum, sources are acknowledged in the bibliography. Any oversight is unintentional and very much regretted.

My special thanks to Lynne Bryer for her invaluable guidance; M D Nash for her ideas on Kipling's writings, which have been incorporated in this book; Dr Ryno Greenwall for allowing me access to his collection; and my family – Max, Andy, Neil and Margaret – for their constant encouragement.

Introduction

South Africa became part of Kipling's life and work for several reasons. His first visit gave him a tantalising glimpse of a subcontinent of great beauty and promise; it was also a place where the British Empire was still visibly expanding. Events began to move inexorably towards the Anglo-Boer confrontation, and when recurring ill health forced his escape from the English winter of 1898, Kipling's choice fell naturally on a portion of the Empire that was rapidly becoming its most vital focus.

At the Cape, friendship with Rhodes – after the Jameson Raid nolong premier, but still the most influential man in the colony – was assured; before long Kipling was offered a place to "hang his hat up", a summer home on Rhodes's mountain slopes. If that were not enough, the outbreak of the Anglo-Boer War in 1899 clinched the matter – the journalist in Kipling could not resist the urge to be on the spot. He began his South African writings with enthusiasm, giving eye-witness accounts of wounded Tommies and brave nurses, and leaping at the change to join the newspaper Lord Roberts set up in a captured Bloemfontein; here he witnessed his first (rather meagre) battle with the Boers. But disillusionment set in as the war dragged on, at enormous cost in lives. Rhodes's death in 1902 was followed by the departure of Jameson and Milner from the political stage; the imperial dream was dwindling. There was nothing to keep Kipling in South Africa, and nothing to keep him writing about it.

Though his Boer war verse forms a sizeable portion of his finer poetry, there are only a few Boer war stories – and Kipling never wrote the South African masterpiece that many were confidently expecting. But whatever its direct literary outcome, the involvement in South African affairs was a crucial phase for Kipling. He was young when the land first engaged his interest; he was in his early forties when events quenched his idealism. He was no longer the poet, rather the critic, of Empire. There is no denying the fascination of these years, nor their importance as a watershed in Kipling's life and art.

Rudyard Kipling at the time of his first brief visit to the Cape in 1981

1 In the hands of Fate

Rudyard Kipling was 26 years old in 1891, the year in which he first saw South Africa, a land whose "colour, light and half-oriental manners" were destined, in his own words, to bind chains round his heart for years to come. But this first visit was brief, part of a sea voyage intended to restore his shaky health, and he was still unaware how much he was "in the hands of Fate" when, on the outward voyage, he met up with a certain Commander Bayly going to Simon's Town, the naval harbour at the Cape.

Cape Town he found "a sleepy, unkempt little place" and, though he appreciated the restorative sunshine and the "dry, spiced smell of the land", there were as yet no indications of the part this corner of the world was to play in his life:

> "How was I to guess that in a few years I should know Simon's Town like the inside of my own pocket, and should give much of my life and love to the glorious land around it?"

Up to this time, the phenomenally successful young author had spent his life between his birthplace, India, and England. At six, Rudyard and his three-year-old sister had been taken to England and left – like many other Anglo-Indian children of their generation – to spend their childhood years with foster parents. The young Rudyard endured five desperately unhappy years at Southsea before his parents were alerted to his misery and sent him as a boarder to the United Services College at Westward Ho! in Devon. At seventeen, Kipling left school and returned to India, where his father, who was principal of an art school and museum curator in Lahore, arranged for him to become assistant editor of the city's *Civil and Military Gazette*.

For the next seven years Kipling coped with a multitude of journalistic tasks fifteen hours a day, six days a week, often in almost unbearable heat. Promotion as a special reporter to the more important Allahabad *Pioneer* in 1887 did not lessen his workload. He edited the magazine supplement and wrote most of the fiction to save the newspaper the expense of authors' serial rights, besides coping with his daily work routine. E. Kay Robinson, Kipling's first editor in Lahore and a lifelong friend, later recalled his youthful exuberance:

> "In the heat of summer, white cotton trousers and a thin vest constituted his office attire, and by the day's end he was spotted all over like a Dalmatian dog. He had a habit of dipping his pen frequently into the inkpot and as all his movements were abrupt, almost jerky, the ink used to fly. When he darted into my room . . . I had to shout to him to stand off, otherwise, as I knew by experience,

Kipling's bookplate (*below*) and one of his volumes of stories for the Indian Railway Library

the abrupt halt he would make, and the flourish with which he placed the proof in his hand before me, would send the penful of ink – he always had a full pen in his hand – flying over me."[1]

Kipling arrived in London in 1889, at the age of 24, and within a year was being acclaimed as one of the most brilliant writers of the day. His literary success had begun with the stories and verses he wrote for the *Civil and Military Gazette*. *Plain Tales from the Hills* and *Departmental Ditties* were published in book form by A H Wheeler & Co, holders of the contract for the Indian Railway bookstalls. Priced at one rupee each, the small books were sold to tourists and travellers throughout India, carrying Kipling's writings far and wide, and were reissued in London by the publishing firm of Sampson Low who took over the English rights.

Kipling's work sometimes verged on gossip-column journalism, but it was fresh and exciting. He put poetry into the mouth of Tommy Atkins, and revealed to the British public the courage, the humour, the stoicism and the loyalty of the common soldier in India.

Not since Dickens had a writer taken so wide a public by storm. Rudyard's sister Alice later recalled:

"Ruddy's success in India was doled out drop by drop; people said, 'Clever young pup!' and talked about his awful side. But in London success came as a flood. It amazed him; he couldn't understand it. He never got a swelled head in the least, even when he received letters – extraordinary letters – from quite cultivated women who wanted to marry him, on or without sight."[2]

In Britain Kipling's name became a household word. *Blackwoods Magazine* suggested that Kipling should be decorated with the Star of India, while the influential literary figure, Edmund Gosse, described him as "a comet flaring across the sky filling the great void in the world of Anglo-Saxon fiction with exotic realism". Henry James, equally impressed but less adulatory, called him "the infant monster of a Kipling".

Kinship on his mother's side with the Burne-Jones, Poynter and Baldwin families, all closely associated with the arts, enabled Kipling to make wide social and literary contacts in London, and he was accepted by all the important writers of the day. A P Watt became his literary agent, an association that was to last a lifetime, and Kipling made a close friend of Wolcott Balestier, a young American visiting London to secure original manuscripts for an American publisher. Balestier, a slightly-built young man with considerable charm and drive, soon enlisted the best English writers, including Kipling, for whom he secured English copyright and American publication for *The Light that Failed*. He also collaborated with Kipling on a novel titled *The Naulahka*, contributing the American chapters. Balestier's rooms in Dean's Yard, Westminster, became a literary centre unparalleled in London at that time.

When Balestier's mother and two sisters joined him in London, his eldest sister Caroline took over the running of his domestic affairs. She and Kipling first met when she visited her brother's office in Dean's Yard; within months there was an understanding between them, though the news was received with little enthusiasm by Rudyard's parents.

Despite this new turn in his life, Kipling realised it was essential for him to get away from London. Twice in India he had broken down from overwork and ill-health. Now, in 1891, "staleness and depression came after a bout of real influenza, when all my Indian microbes joined hands and sang for a month in the darkness of Villiers Street". So the trip to the southern hemisphere – South Africa, New Zealand and Australia, then "home" to India – was arranged. Kipling sailed from Southampton in the *Mexican* (not, as he later recalled in his autobiography, the *Moor*) on 22 August 1891, arriving in Cape Town on the morning of 10 September. During the 19-day voyage to the Cape, the passengers shared one principal topic of conversation: Cecil Rhodes, Prime Minister of the Cape Colony, whose achievements had caught the imagination of people all over the world.

Now a statesman and financier of international repute, Rhodes had emigrated from Britain to South Africa in 1870 as a young man of delicate health, to join his eldest brother in a cotton growing venture in Natal. When their first crop failed, the two brothers moved to the diamond-fields of Kimberley. Here Rhodes quickly mastered the diamond business, formed the De Beers Mining Company in 1880, and made enough money to take a degree at Oxford the following year. When gold was discovered on the Witwatersrand in 1886, he became a prospector but soon formed his own gold-mining company, Consolidated Gold Fields of South Africa.

A Union Castle steamship in the Cape Town docks of 1900

Rhodes made his entry into southern African politics in 1881 when he was elected to the Cape Colony's House of Assembly, a position he was to hold all his life. As his love of Africa deepened, he dreamed of a new British empire on the African continent, and conceived the idea of a South African federation, governing itself within the Empire and extending far into Africa. When the British government awarded his British South Africa Company extraordinary power and authority over an enormous area of southern Africa in 1889, his dream came close to realisation. Rhodes reached the crowning point of his career in 1890 when he was elected Prime Minister of the Cape Colony. A financier whose versatility, strength, negotiating abilities and generosity were renowned in Britain – where he was offered almost unlimited capital for his projects – he was admired for his ability to be as much at ease with a Dutch politician in the Colony as with a prince at home.

Kipling was to catch a glimpse of Rhodes in a Cape Town restaurant, but was not destined to meet the Prime Minister on this first visit, as Rhodes left Cape Town for a visit to Beira on 14 September, shortly after Kipling's arrival.

Kipling spent two weeks in Cape Town, where he found his fame had preceded him. "At some future day we may have the pleasure of hearing what he thinks of the

Karoo, the Cape Town Malay, Kimberley's big diamond-hole and the Rand," declared *The Cape Argus* on the day he landed. Although he originally intended to visit Kimberley, Kipling instead travelled no further than the Karoo village of Matjiesfontein to visit Olive Schreiner, whose *Story of an African Farm* he much admired. He had first met her at the Mowbray home of Sir Thomas Ekins Fuller, general manager of the Union Steamship Company and one of four Cape Town representatives in the Cape Colony's House of Assembly, and had offered her his help in getting her next book published.

At the Cape, Kipling was particularly fascinated by the British naval station:

> "My Navy Captain introduced me to the Naval society of Simon's Town, where the south-easter blows five days a week, and the Admiral of the Cape Station lived in splendour, with at least a brace of live turtles harnessed to the end of a little wooden jetty, swimming about till due to be taken up for turtle soup. The Navy Club there and the tales of the junior officers delighted me beyond words. There I witnessed one of the most comprehensive 'rags' I had ever seen. It rose out of a polite suggestion to a newly-appointed Lieutenant-Commander that the foretopmast of his tiny gunboat 'wanted staying forward'. It went on till all the furniture was completely rearranged all over the room."

The 'rag' inspired a short story, "Judson and the Empire", published in *Many Inventions* in 1893. This tale of "a wallowing wash-tub" of a gunboat, commanded by a young officer with a flair for diplomacy, begins and ends in Simon's Town.

A recurrence of his malaria temporarily soured Kipling's view of South Africa, yet he did not escape its spell. Ten years and two visits later, he was to write:

Olive Schreiner was in her mid-thirties when Kipling met her. She was living in a cottage (*below*) in the Karoo, seeking relief in that dry climate from the asthma that plagued her. When she married in 1894, Kipling sent her a full set of his writings; they were to meet again in South Africa in 1898.

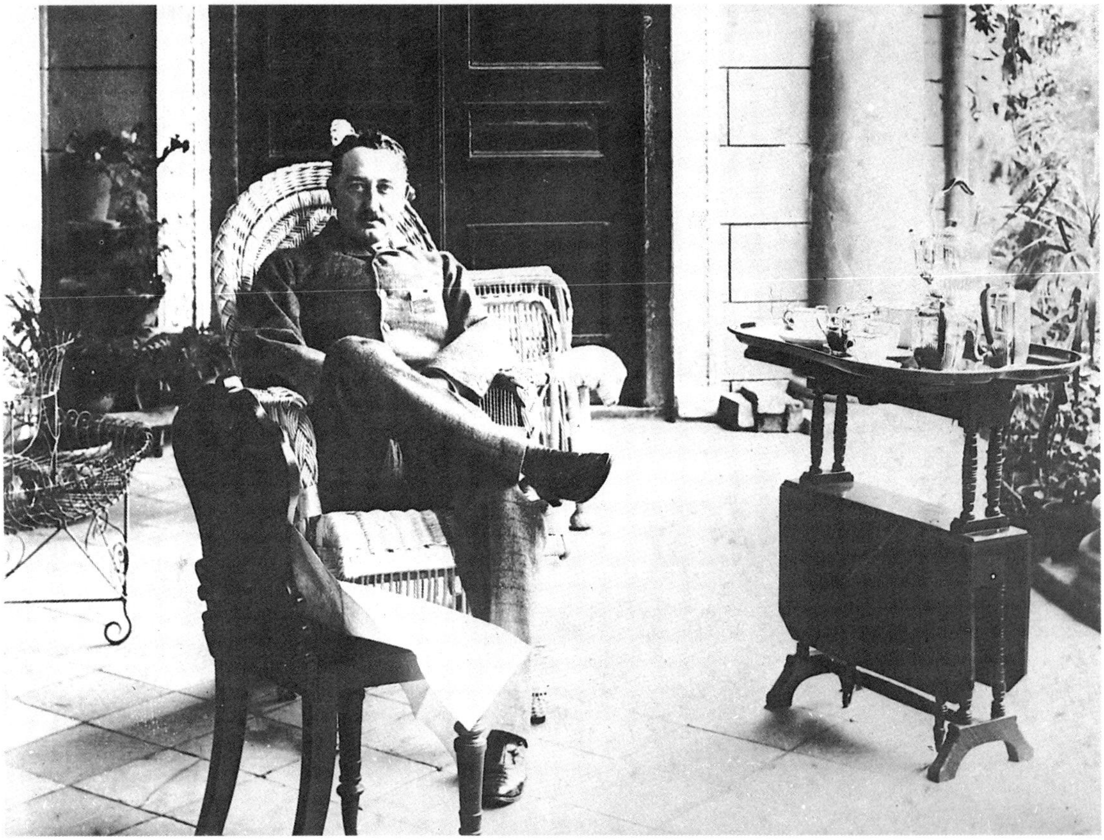

CJ Rhodes, imperialist, mining magnate and Cape premier (photographed here at his palatial home, Groote Schuur), was destined to play a major role in Kipling's life.

> "A man lay sick of a fever under Table Mountain, persuaded that, of all vile lands, South Africa was the worst. But wiser men than he said between the quinine doses:- 'You'll come back again. When it's all over you'll long to come back again.' They were entirely right. The man hankered to see more of the fascinating country, and in due course of years back he came to fall in love with heath, dysa (disa), plumbago, the sudden flush of bloom in the karroo after rain, the thunderstorms among the ironstone hills, and the big, dry distances of the North."[3]

For the next leg of his southern travels, Kipling joined the *Doric* when it sailed for Wellington, New Zealand, on 25 September 1891. The long sea voyage inspired one of his most vividly expressive poems, "M'Andrew's Hymn" *(The Seven Seas)*. It is mainly a celebration of the marvel of machinery, but Kipling gave a nod to the Cape as he sailed east:

We'll tak' one stretch – three weeks an' odd by ony road ye steer –
Fra' Cape Town east to Wellington – ye need an engineer . . .

Kipling arrived in Wellington on 18 October; before leaving on a tour of the springs and geysers in the Hot Lakes district, he told a press interviewer that he had been immediately struck with South Africa, and regretted he could not stay there longer:

> "It is a most fascinating place. There is an empire behind Cape Town. Already they have a railway line a hundred miles into the interior. There are almost unlimited future possibilities for that South African empire. No one can say what its future is to be, but it must be something big. People do not realise yet what Africa means to the world. Then more will be heard yet about the native races. They are men who will fight and breed, too. There is no dying out before the white man about them."[4]

Kipling reached Auckland on 28 October. It was the briefest of visits, but there he came across a widowed hotel keeper round whom, some years later, he was to conjure the complex and enigmatic story of "Mrs Bathurst" which he included in *Traffics and Discoveries*, and which he set in Simon's Town.

Kipling's next port of call was Melbourne; he spent less than two weeks in Australia, travelling to Sydney and Adelaide before sailing in the P & O liner *Valetta* for Colombo on 25 November. A long train journey through southern and central India brought him to Lahore a week before Christmas.

With his parents and sister about to leave Lahore and return to England for good,

Simon's Town, naval harbour of the Cape, as Kipling knew it.

The Royal Navy Club at Simon's Town (*left*), where the tales of junior officers delighted Kipling. The story "Judson of the Empire" and the later "Mrs Bathurst" are set in this naval milieu.

Right: Carrie Kipling with the three children in 1898 – John (the baby), Elsie at centre, and Kipling's beloved Josephine, whom they were to lose the following year. The story "They" sprang from the sorrow of this experience.

it was to be Kipling's last visit to India – and the only real home he had known. In Lahore he had hardly settled down to the warmth of the "family square", as his mother liked to call the foursome, when he received a cable from Caroline Balestier with the news that her brother Wolcott, his beloved friend and literary collaborator, had died of typhoid fever in Dresden. Rudyard left Lahore immediately, stopping only in Bombay to see his old ayah, and was back in London by January 1892 to give what solace he could to the Balestier family.

Brought close together by their love of Wolcott and a shared grief, Rudyard and Caroline were married in London on the 18th of January in a quiet ceremony. Since Carrie's mother was seriously ill with influenza, there was no reception and the ceremony was attended by only a handful of close friends. Rudyard's cousin Ambrose Poynter was the best man, and Henry James gave away the bride.

After a honeymoon tour of America, Japan and Canada, Rudyard and Carrie returned to America to settle at Brattleboro in Vermont, where Carrie's family owned property and had lived for many years. Here, with the help of Carrie's younger brother Beatty, the Kiplings built their first home, Naulakha, and here their first daughter, Josephine, was born on 29 December 1892.

There were many visitors to Naulakha: Kipling's father arrived before the house was completed, Carrie's mother spent a Christmas with them; and Conan Doyle brought his golf clubs and gave Kipling lessons in a field. Later Kipling, sustaining a Glasgow accent throughout, read him the first draft of "M'Andrew's Hymn". Frank N Doubleday of Scribner's visited Naulakha too, paying Kipling the record American price of 500 dollars for "M'Andrew's Hymn". But the Kiplings made few local friends – although Josephine's birth introduced them to Dr James Conland who became a close friend. Rudyard was happy to spend a great deal of time with his daughter, to whom he was devoted.

In 1894 the Kiplings visited their parents in their new home in England. In the London season of that year, Kipling's fame was considerably enhanced when his portrait appeared in *Vanity Fair*, and he was a guest at many prestigious functions, including a dinner given in his and Lord Roberts' honour. For Kipling this was truly an accolade: as a young man in India, he had known and admired the great soldier from afar.

During the time he lived at Brattleboro, Kipling produced some of his finest work: the two *Jungle Books*, which appeared in 1894 and 1895; a miscellany of short stories in the volume *The Day's Work*; a second set of *Barrack-room Ballads*; and a selection of verses collected in *The Seven Seas*. For the verse, as always, he hummed and tapped out the rhythms. "When he had got a tune into his head," his old friend, E. Kay

Robinson said, "the words and rhyme came as readily as when a singer vamps his own banjo accompaniment."[5]

The Kipling's second daughter, Elsie, was born at Brattleboro in February 1896. But these happy days in America were flawed by the considerable ill-feeling that was growing between the couple and Beatty Balestier and his wife. Finally an unpleasant incident occurred when Kipling fell off his bicycle and was almost run over by his brother-in-law on horseback; Beatty brandished a whip and let flow a stream of insults and bad language. Unwisely, Kipling charged his brother-in-law with threats of murder. Beatty was arrested, brought before the Justice of the Peace and remanded on bail until the next session of the County Court.

In the glare of unpleasant publicity which followed this incident, the Kiplings went into seclusion. Their peace at Naulakha had been shattered, and they made the difficult decision to pack up and leave Vermont. Before the remanded trial could take place, they had left for England.

Although Rudyard never liked their first English home at Maidencombe near Torquay, it was here that he began to make his name as a serious writer. At the age of 32 he was elected to the Athenaeum Club, becoming one of its youngest members. On the day of his admission, he dined with the editor of *The Times* and two new acquaintances who would soon play an important part in his life: Sir Alfred Milner and Cecil Rhodes.

Left: The impressive bulk of Rhodes matched the weight of his obsession with the dream of uniting Africa under the British flag. After Rhodes's fall from grace, John Buchan commented on his "huge but crippled power" (*Memory hold the Door*).

Right: Sir Alfred (later Lord) Milner, at the time Kipling first met him in London. A mutual regard for Rhodes ensured their friendship.

Milner, whose competence in academic, financial and political affairs had been recognised by the British government, had made a close study of South Africa while working on the *Pall Mall Gazette*, and he was about to leave England to take up his appointment as Governor of the Cape Colony and High Commissioner for South Africa.

The dinner reawakened Kipling's interest in South Africa and offered him the long awaited opportunity to meet Rhodes. Though no longer Prime Minister of the Cape Colony, Rhodes was still a Member of Parliament and an entrepreneur now largely devoting his energies to the development of white settlement in Rhodesia, and the establishment of agricultural estates in the Cape Colony. Both personally and politically, Rhodes was to become a major influence in Kipling's life and work. Kipling believed implicitly that the British had a greater aptitude for ruling than other people, and a civilising mission to "take up the white man's burden"; his own task was to translate the ideals and emotions underlying this imperial trusteeship into art. Rudyard was to find the perfect exemplar of his imperial ideas in Rhodes.

In 1897, with Carrie expecting their third child, house-hunting in Kent and Sussex took precedence over all Rudyard's and Carrie's other affairs. The Kiplings had spent nine months in Maidencombe, and found damp winter months there unbearable. Lady Georgiana Burne-Jones, Kipling's Aunt Georgie, offered them the use of North End House, the Burne-Jones' seaside home at Rottingdean near Brighton. Though Aunt Georgie and Kipling always argued about politics, their affection for each other was deep and constant. At her suggestion, the Kiplings decided they would remain in North End House until the birth, before renting a nearby house called The Elms.

While they were still at North End House, Kipling was encouraged by *The Times* to write an ode in celebration of Queen Victoria's Diamond Jubilee; he produced "Recessional". Not a man to write to order, he only completed the poem on Jubilee Day – and almost immediately consigned it to the wastepaper basket. Retrieved by Aunt Georgie and a friend, "Recessional" was printed in *The Times* on 17 July 1897, accompanied by a paragraph of approval in the leading article. The poem received inordinate praise. "It is the greatest poem that has been written by any living man," said Sir Edward Clarke, the distinguished QC and Member of Parliament, and thousands of people agreed with him as they read the stirring imperialist message:

God of our fathers, known of old,
Lord of our far-flung battle-line,
Beneath whose awful Hand we hold
Dominion over palm and pine –
Lord God of Hosts, be with us yet,
Lest we forget – lest we forget!

Kipling accepted no payment for "Recessional"; although some of his poems over the years received generous three figure sums, there were certain verses which appeared in *The Times* – all his South African verse, for example – for which he would never take payment.

Inevitably, there was some bitterness about "Recessional". "Mr Kipling," the novelist George Moore observed from Dublin, "would not have written the most hideous verses ever written in a beautiful language if he had not lived in a specially hideous moment – the moment of the African millionaire." In Moore's opinion, the verses were "a disgraceful blot on the most beautiful poetic record in the world".[6] But Moore's views were not shared by the mass of Kipling's readers. Though he had intimated as early as 1895 that he would decline to be poet laureate if the post were offered to him, there is little doubt that by 1897 Rudyard Kipling was widely regarded as the unofficial poet laureate of the British Empire.

2 The life unaltered

John, the Kiplings' son, was born on 17 August 1897 at North End House, Rottingdean. In September the family moved across the green to The Elms, which they rented – not altogether happily – while Rudyard, all the autumn, searched for a house to buy.

The search was unsuccessful, and in December Kipling wrote to his old friend Dr Conland in Vermont:

> "I've been rather out of sorts. Hipped and depressed from day to day and this climate does not help to put a man on his legs again when he once feels sorrowful . . . We are all off to South Africa to play about in the sunshine until April. Cape Town is the paradise for children . . . Josephine tells me that the best way of studying geography is 'to go about in ships, Father, till you have seen them all', and frankly I am somewhat of her way of thinking . . . My father is coming down with us for the trip . . ."[1]

Kipling and the children John and Elsie in the garden of The Elms, the house (*right*) in which they lived from 1896 to 1902. From 1898 they avoided English winters by summering at the Cape.

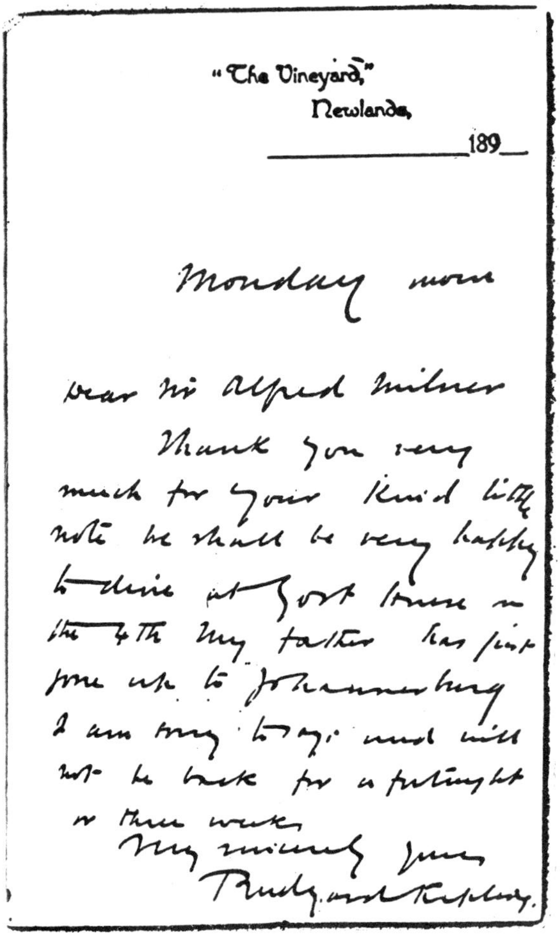
"The Vineyard,"
Newlands,
189__

Monday morn

Dear Sir Alfred Milner
Thank you very much for your kind little note we shall be very happy to dine at Govt House on the 4th. My father has just gone up to Johannesburg I am sorry to say: and will not be back for a fortnight or three weeks.
Very sincerely yours
Rudyard Kipling.

Left: Reply from Kipling to Milner's invitation to dine at Government House, Cape Town, 1898. A new friend was Edmund Garrett (*below*), youthful editor of the *Cape Times.*

For practical advice on where to stay in Cape Town and "the methods and manners of housekeeping down there", Kipling consulted friend and fellow-member of the Savile Club, Rider Haggard, whose five years in South Africa had inspired a succession of phenomenally popular novels, beginning with *King Solomon's Mines.* (Kipling acknowledged that it was a chance sentence in one of Haggard's romances, *Nada the Lily,* that had started him on the track that led to the *Jungle Books.*) Their common interest in South Africa made an early bond between the two writers, who met and corresponded regularly until Haggard's death.

On 8 January 1898 Kipling, his wife, his father and the three children, accompanied by a nursemaid and a governess, embarked at Southampton in the *Dunvegan Castle* for Cape Town. John Hays Hammond, consulting engineer to Cecil Rhodes, was a passenger in the same ship and found the Kiplings to be excellent travelling companions. "Rudyard manifested his 'satiable curtiosity'," Hammond noticed, "by prowling endlessly from engine room to bridge getting information which, as he said, he filed away in his memory for future use."[2]

By February 1898, after a brief stay in the Vineyard Hotel in Newlands, the Kipling ménage was settled in Mrs Trotter's boarding house in the same leafy suburb on the slopes of Table Mountain. Although their accommodation was not without its drawbacks – Kipling complained that their hostess spread "miseries and discomforts round her in return for good monies" – the family was enchanted by Cape Town. The dry heat and the gentle servants reminded Kipling of his early years in India:

We shall go back by the boltless doors,
To the life unaltered our childhood knew –
To the naked feet on the cool, dark floors,
And the high-ceiled rooms that the Trade blows through:

To the trumpet-flowers and the moon beyond,
And the three-toad's chorus drowning all –
And the lisp of the split banana-frond
That talked us to sleep when we were small.

The wayside magic, the threshold spells,
Shall soon undo what the North has done –
Because of the sights and the sounds and the smells
That ran with our youth in the eye of the sun.

(*"Song of the Wise Children"*, *The Five Nations*)

The long summer evenings and the ready hospitality of Cape society made it easy for the Kiplings to forge new friendships, among them Edmund Garrett, the editor of the *Cape Times*, in whose offices Kipling liked to spend several hours every Tuesday, when the overseas mail arrived. His comments frequently ended up as the basis for leading articles.

Kipling's interest in Cape politics was keen from the start, so that it was no surprise that his circle in Cape Town included the two most important Englishmen in South Africa (whom he had already met in London): Cecil Rhodes, and the recently appointed High Commissioner for British South Africa, Sir Alfred Milner.

Milner, a young man in his early forties, was unreservedly committed to the Imperial cause. Yet in the tradition of the English proconsuls, he handled the tense South African situation dispassionately and with restraint. Kipling had been an admirer of Milner long before they lunched together at the Athenaeum. Now, although Milner was shackled by his official duties and had little time to relax in Kipling's company, they succeeded in establishing an enduring bond of fellow feeling.

Kipling's renewed acquaintance with Rhodes was the beginning of a close friendship that lasted until the day the statesman died. "What's your dream?" Rhodes blurted out at one of their early meetings; Kipling replied that Rhodes was part of it.

Handicapped by the inability to express himself in words, Rhodes was, Kipling discovered, as tongue-tied as a schoolboy of fifteen. "My use to him was mainly as a purveyor of words; for he was largely inarticulate. After the idea had been presented – and one had to know his code for it – he would say: 'What am I trying to express? Say it, *say* it!' So I would say it, and if the phrase suited not, he would work it over, chin a little down, till it satisfied him." And then Kipling would often concur, without question, with the thought or opinion he had helped to structure.

Rhodes, who was now a multi-millionaire, was using his fortune to build up a new and greater British Empire in southern Africa – he had a vision of a united South Africa, with railway and telegraphic communication from the Cape to Cairo. Since he was no longer Premier of the Cape, he had time for a host of projects. The disastrous Jameson Raid of 1895 had ruined his political career and he bitterly regretted it. As a result of this debacle, the political dividing lines between English and Afrikaner in the Cape had become more sharply drawn. The Afrikaner Bond, the conservative Cape Afrikaner party, withdrew the support it had lent Rhodes and became representative of exclusively Afrikaner sentiment and aspirations. "I blundered," Rhodes told Sir James McDonald, his agent in Rhodesia and his frequent companion on the veld, "God, how badly I blundered, but . . . I am not going to give in, I shall continue to work for South Africa harder than ever."[3]

With enormous enthusiasm Rhodes pored over maps, charts, books and catalogues at Groote Schuur, the beautiful estate at Rondebosch that he had acquired when he was Prime Minister. There was much on Rhodes's mind: irrigation schemes, progressive stock and fruit farming, and the germ of the great scholarship scheme that he had believed would help to safeguard the peace of the world. He took Kipling to Paarl to show him his fruit farms, with the wonderful old Dutch houses "stalled in deep peace". Here, in the middle of an orchard of apple trees, was Lekkerwijn, the home of Rhodes's manager, with its beautiful oak furniture and fine Dutch ironware and silver. Kipling and Rhodes spent a few days in the house, where Kipling was moved to carve a poem into the drawing-room mantelpiece:

This is the blossom of the fruit.
I cleared the land, I set the trees;
I led the water down the sluit.
Earth gave me fiftyfold increase –
This is the blossom of the fruit.[4]

Rhodes as colossus – pith helmet in hand, he straddles Africa "from Cape to Cairo" in this *Punch* cartoon of 1892. In fact, his "empire" reached no further than the land that was named Rhodesia after him.

Opposite: The imposing verandah of Groote Schuur, Rhodes's home on the slopes of Table Mountain.

Carrie stayed with the children at the Cape for the whole four months of their visit, but in the last weeks before the voyage home, Rhodes arranged for Kipling to visit Rhodesia, which had recently been made accessible by railway. In Bulawayo, Kipling – an enthusiastic cyclist – explored the town on a hired bicycle. The proprietor of the only cycle shop had been so unimpressed by the "scruffy little fellow" dressed in khaki trousers that he sent him off to find a guarantor before he would hire him a machine. Kipling returned accompanied by Rhodes himself.

The incident did not detract from Kipling's favourable impression of the town. He told the Bulawayo correspondent of a London paper: "I have some small knowledge of new towns and the impression I've gathered is that there's no point on which any one of them can compare with this city . . ." "Then you're going home to tell the public all about us in 'Plain Tales from the Veld'?" suggested the reporter. Kipling shook his head: "No, no, nothing of the kind . . . I am not here for work and am fairly at sea in these parts."[5]

On his return journey to Cape Town in April 1898, Kipling stopped off in Johannesburg to attend a banquet given in his honour at the Rand Club, haunt of the mining magnates and Uitlander figures of the day. Among the sixty-four men present was Percy FitzPatrick, erstwhile prospector and transport rider who as a member of the "Reform Committee" had been arrested after the abortive Jameson Raid. He struck up an enduring friendship with Kipling, who was frequently a visitor at the spacious FitzPatrick home, Hohenheim; it was here that Kipling was to hear his host

Kipling's literary friendships in South Africa included Percy Fitz-Patrick (*left*), author of *Jock of the Bushveld*, and Olive Schreiner – who hated Rhodes but wrote of Kipling (*below*) as a "real man, a most loveable little creature".

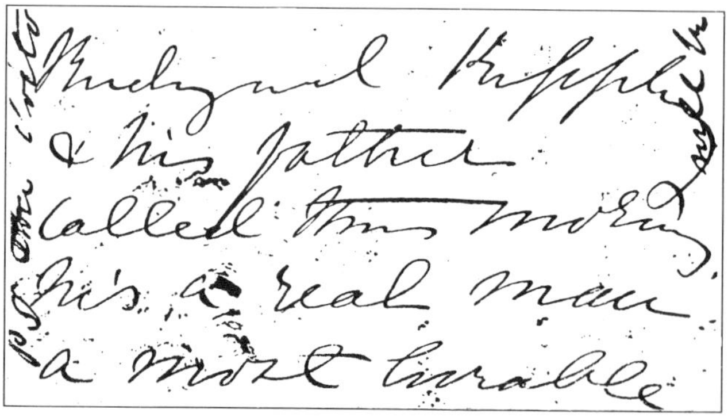

Rudyard Kipling
& his father
called this morning.
He's a real man
a most lovable

relating his pioneer experiences in the Bushveld with his dog. The stories were bed-time tales for the FitzPatrick children, but Kipling was quick to recognise their merit and urged his friend to write them down. *Jock of the Bushveld*, a South African classic, appeared in 1907.

With his father, who had come up from Cape Town, Kipling next paid a brief visit to Kimberley. Here he spent time with Olive Schreiner, who had moved to the town in search of relief from the asthma which troubled her constantly. She wrote to a friend of the visit: "We've seen a good deal of Rudyard Kipling these last days. He's lovable." To her brother she repeated the epithet: ". . . He's a real man, a most love-able little human creature."[6] But neither she nor Kipling appear to have left any record of what they discussed, an unusual and regrettable omission in the case of two famous writers.

Back at the Cape, a general election was in the offing, with the English-speaking Progressive Party opposing the more moderate South African Party. The Kiplings took their seats on the platform at a pre-election meeting where Rhodes spoke in support of the Progressive candidates. (In the event, the South African Party, with the support of the Afrikaner Bond, were to succeed by a narrow margin in coming into office.)

April's shorter days and cooler evenings signalled the end of the Kiplings' summer holiday. It was time for the portmanteaux and trunks to be packed and the many farewells to be made before the entourage left Cape Town in the *Norham Castle*, bound for Southampton.

One of the most nervous guests at Kipling's farewell dinner at the City Club was a 23 year old private in the army medical corps at Simon's Town who wrote verses modelled on the style of Kipling's "Barrack-room Ballads". The editor of the *Cape Times* had asked the young man – whose name was Edgar Wallace – to provide a

"Welcome to Kipling" poem for the writer's arrival in South Africa, and the imitation had caught Kipling's attention. Now, meeting its youthful perpetrator, he extended a friendly warning: "For God's sake, don't take to literature as a profession. Literature is a splendid mistress, but a bad wife!"[7] Though for some years to come Wallace concentrated on journalism, he ultimately ignored Kipling's humorous advice and went on to become one of the most successful crime writers of all time.

The Kipling's return to Rottingdean signalled a series of family crises. The summer of 1898 saw the death of Sir Edward Burne Jones, Kipling's uncle, to whom he had always been close. Rudyard and Carrie began to spend as much time as possible with the widowed Aunt Georgie. At the end of the year Kipling's sister Alice, who had recently returned to England from India with her husband, suffered a nervous breakdown and was sent to be nursed at her parents' home in Tisbury.

Rudyard was anxious to see a New York publisher about a copyright dispute, and Carrie wanted to visit her mother. In spite of the severe winter, the Kiplings decided to spend a holiday in America in January 1899. The voyage across the Atlantic was particularly stormy and cold. By the time the family landed in New York, the two little girls had serious colds which later developed into whooping cough. The whole family seemed to be dogged with ill-health. Carrie went down with fever, Rudyard developed a lung inflammation which induced delirium, and Josephine's condition worsened as her temperature rose alarmingly.

Kipling was kind to aspiring young writer Edgar Wallace, whom he later recommended as a war correspondent in the Anglo-Boer War (*see cartoon right*).

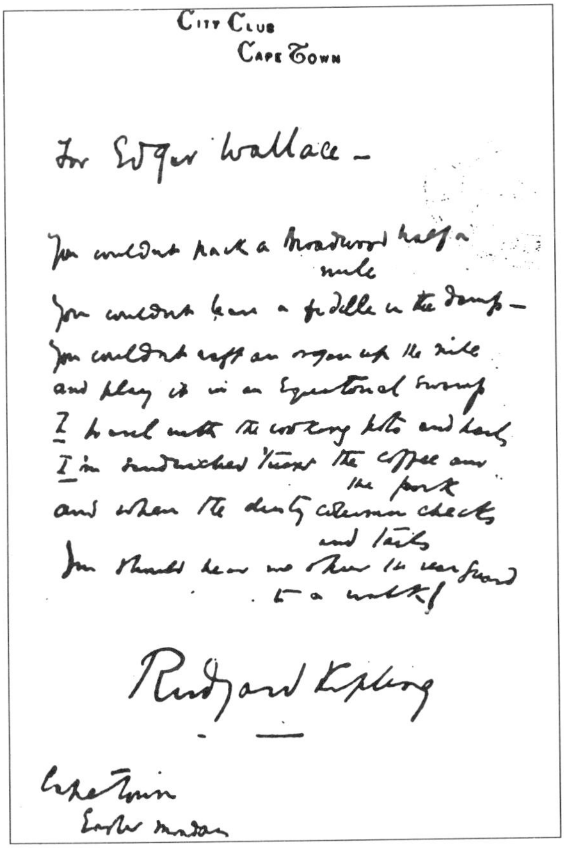
City Club
Cape Town

For Edgar Wallace –

You couldn't pack a Broadwood half a mile
You couldn't leave a fiddle in the damp –
You couldn't raft an organ up the Nile
and play it in an Equatorial swamp
I travel with the cooking pots and pails
I'm sandwiched 'tween the coffee and the pork
and when the dusty column checks and tails
You should hear me spur the rear guard to a walk!

Rudyard Kipling

Cape Town
Easter Monday

This 1899 portrait of Kipling (*above left*), by Strang, reveals how deeply loss had etched the writer's face. Yet he was still a fun-loving father to John and Elsie, sketched playfully on board the *Kinfauns Castle*, 1900.

Rudyard's illness was headline news all over the world. People everywhere waited for bulletins on his progress. At the Hotel Grenoble in New York, where the family were staying with three doctors in attendance, crowds of people blocked traffic in the street, reporters constantly pestered Carrie for news, and people from every walk of life extended their sympathy. Suddenly Rudyard rallied and his doctors declared him out of danger. But Josephine, struck by the same illness as her father, did not have his reserves of strength. Early in the morning of a cold March day she died.

Rudyard convalesced slowly. In June his doctors agreed that the family could return home, but ordered him to avoid spending any more winters in England. Neither Rudyard nor Carrie ever recovered from their daughter's death. The loss of Josephine, whom Rudyard had loved intensely, was beyond bearing. Even Rottingdean had lost its charm; there were constant memories of Josephine in the house and in the garden.

Kipling was now at the height of his fame and the family had a new predicament to contend with: visitors to the neighbourhood who stopped to stare at the celebrity and his home, while whole charabancs of sightseers regularly congregated at the gates of the house. It was time to begin looking for a new home as far away as possible from prying trippers. But it was not to be until 1902 – after considerable travelling between England and South Africa – that the Kiplings were to find their ideal home.

3 Gentlemen in khaki

Kipling had been fighting for his life in New York in the winter of 1899. In South Africa, the political situation was deteriorating swiftly. As Rudyard recuperated during the English summer, he grew increasingly concerned at the news from the Transvaal (the Zuid-Afrikaansche Republiek) of growing dissension between President Kruger and the Uitlanders.

Determined to preserve Boer paramountcy and keep the Transvaal independent of British influence, Kruger had imposed a 14-year residence qualification which withheld citizenship from the thousands of Uitlanders (foreigners), most of them British subjects, who had flocked to the goldfields. The majority of the Republic's population, who paid five-sixths of its taxes, were thus denied a voice in its government. Tension had been increased by the Jameson Raid, the abortive Uitlander attempt to depose Kruger by force at the end of 1895.

After four years of growing Uitlander frustration, in April 1899 a petition setting out these grievances and appealing for intervention was presented to the Queen of England. When asked for his views, Milner telegraphed his grandiloquent "Helots' Dispatch", alleging that the case for intervention was overwhelming: "The spectacle of thousands of British subjects kept permanently in the position of helots . . . does steadily undermine the influence and reputation of Great Britain." Four months of fruitless diplomatic negotiations were to follow, while the Transvaal prepared for war.

Twelve thousand British troops were already in South Africa, and a further ten thousand were sent out in September 1899. The governments of the Transvaal and her sister republic and ally, the Orange Free State, issued orders to mobilise their fighting commandos. The Uitlander exodus from Johannesburg and Pretoria became a panic. On the eve of war, Kipling's poem "The Old Issue" was published in *The Times*. It denounced Kruger as "sloven, sullen, savage, secret, uncontrolled" and placed the Uitlander struggle in the historical English tradition of resistance to tyranny and autocratic rule:

All we have of freedom, all we use or know –
This our fathers bought for us long and long ago.

Ancient Right unnoticed as the breath we draw –
Leave to live by no man's leave, underneath the Law –

Lance and torch and tumult, steel and grey-goose wing,
Wrenched it, inch and ell and all, slowly from the King.

* * *

Paul Kruger, Transvaal president and ageing patriarch, photographed with his staff in the fateful year 1899, a few months before the outbreak of the Anglo-Boer War. He died abroad, in exile in Switzerland, in 1904.

We shall drink dishonour, we shall eat abuse
For the Land we look to – for the Tongue we use.

We shall take our station, dirt beneath his feet,
While his hired captains jeer us in the street.

Cruel in the shadow, crafty in the sun,
Far beyond his borders shall his teachings run.

On the day the British reinforcements reached the port of Durban, Kruger issued an ultimatum to the British Government to withdraw its troops from Boer frontiers and return the reinforcements to England. The Queen's rejection of these demands was cabled to South Africa on 10 October 1899; on the following day the Boer Republics declared war.

Kipling believed his country had no choice but to go to war:

Now, this is the faith that the White Men hold
When they build their homes afar –
"Freedom for ourselves and freedom for our sons
And, failing freedom, War."

In October, shortly after war was declared, Kipling was invited to address a meeting of the Imperial South African Association at Brighton. This body, of which he was an active member, had been founded "to uphold British supremacy and to promote the interests of British subjects in South Africa" by disseminating information through meetings and publications. Kipling could not attend in person, but he sent a message to be read out in his absence:

> "I am entirely in sympathy with the object of the meeting and realise our country's obligation at this crisis, to support Her Majesty's Government unreservedly. Their demand, I take it, will be for equal rights for all white men from the Cape to Zambesi, their aim the establishment of a Republic instead of an oligarchy, and their vindication a new and regenerate Transvaal governed under equal laws framed in open council by free men, neither corrupted nor coerced, representing every interest in the land. These things are good and desirable, and I recognise that it is the duty of each one of us, according to his abilities, to work towards their attainment."[1]

The *Daily Mail*, aware of Kipling's immense influence, offered him £10 000 to represent the paper in South Africa as a war correspondent. But Kipling felt he could not undertake such a task. His immediate contribution to the war effort was a set of verses, "The Absent-minded Beggar", that was published in the *Daily Mail* of 31 October 1899 with the express aim of raising money for the Soldiers' Families Fund. The *Daily Mail* proprietor, Alfred Harmsworth, had himself asked Kipling to make the appeal for funds, partly as a circulation-booster for the paper.

Caton Woodville's sketch of "a gentleman in kharki" illustrated Kipling's lyrics for the fund-raising Boer war song "The Absent-minded Beggar" (1899). The song's popularity was so enormous that the image of the bandaged Tommy became a cliché of the war. Proceeds from the sale of the song-sheet/poem (*see page 32*) were "devoted by the *Daily Mail* in the name of Rudyard Kipling, to the benefit of the wives and children of the Reservists".

The Absent-Minded Beggar

When you've shouted "Rule Britannia" – when you've sung "God save the Queen" –
When you've finished killing Kruger with your mouth –
Will you kindly drop a shilling in my little tambourine
For a gentleman in kharki ordered South?
He's an absent-minded beggar and his weaknesses are great –
But we and Paul must take him as we find him –
He is out on active service, wiping something off a slate –
And he's left a lot o' little things behind him!

Duke's son – cook's son – son of a hundred Kings –
(Fifty thousand horse and foot going to Table Bay!)
Each of 'em doing his country's work (and who's to look after their things?)
Pass the hat for your credit's sake, and – pay! pay! pay!

There are families by thousands, far too proud to beg or speak –
And they'll put their sticks and bedding up the spout,
And they'll live on half o' nothing paid 'em punctual once a week,
'Cause the man that earned the wage is ordered out.
He's an absent-minded beggar, but he heard his country call,
And his reg'ment didn't need to send to find him:
He chucked his job and joined it – so the job before us all
Is to help the home that Tommy's left behind him!

Duke's job – cook's job – gardener, baronet, groom –
Mews or palace or paper-shop – there's someone gone away!
Each of 'em doing his country's work (and who's to look after the room?)
Pass the hat for your credit's sake, and – pay! pay! pay!

Let us manage so as later we can look him in the face,
And tell him – what he'd very much prefer –
That, while he saved the Empire his employer saved his place,
And his mates (that's you and me) looked out for her.
He's an absent-minded beggar, and he may forget it all,
But we do not want his kiddies to remind him
That we sent 'em to the workhouse while their daddy hammered Paul,
So we'll help the homes our Tommy's left behind him!

Cook's home – Duke's home – home of a millionaire.
(Fifty thousand horse and foot going to Table Bay!)
Each of 'em doing his country's work (and what have you got to spare?)
Pass the hat for your credit's sake, and – pay! pay! pay!

Spy

Previous page: Kipling "arrives" with his *Vanity Fair* portrait, 1894.

Left: Rhodes in the grounds of Groote Schuur. The house (*top*) was placed so that its marble-flagged verandah faced up the mountain for Rhodes's favourite view. The dining room (*above*) was the scene of many dinners where Kipling met what he called the "interesting folk" of the day.

Above: A rural Cape cottage on one of the fruit farms Rhodes had established in the Paarl district beyond Cape Town. Kipling said: "It was his wish and his will that there should be a fruit-growing industry in the Colony".

Vanity Fair cartoon of Kruger complete with pipe, Bible, top hat and umbrella (*left*).

Right: A rare portrait of Kipling during the Anglo-Boer War, seated bareheaded among the war correspondents with whom he worked in Bloemfontein.

Spy

Opposite: Spy's 1901 cartoon of Lord Roberts (*left*) celebrates the spry hero of the campaign in South Africa. A sorrowing Kruger is cast in grey rock.

Above: This French caricature of Monsieur Cecil Rhodes bears the bitter inscription "L'Argent, cést le sang des autres" (Gold is the blood of others), placing the blame for the war squarely on his shoulders.

Above: The bandaged Tommy of "The Absent-Minded Beggar" cropped up on countless objects that have become collector's items among Boer war memorabilia, like this paper knife and card case (*left*) and statuette.

Left: Another cartoon of Rhodes, this time from *The Struwwelpeter Alphabet* (1900), depicting his downfall due to the Jameson Raid of 1895.

The newspaper's first reaction to the verses was far from enthusiastic, and Sir Arthur Sullivan, when approached to set them to music, claimed he found it difficult to do anything with such "uninspiring" material. But when Sullivan conducted the finished song in London's packed Alhambra Theatre on the night of 13 November, the audience went wild. Everyone joined in the chorus, and within a few days "The Absent-minded Beggar" was the only tune to be heard in England. Lillie Langtry contributed £100 to the fund for the privilege of singing the song on stage, and Lady Tree, wife of the well-known actor-manager, recited the verses daily for 14 weeks at the Palace Theatre and raised £70 000 for the fund.

The song was sung and played in music halls, at smoking concerts and drawing-room recitals, and cranked out on barrel-organs all over the country. Thousands of copies were rushed through the press. The words were printed on every kind of paper and on silk, satin and linen, and the famous Caton Woodville illustration of a wounded Tommy appeared on tobacco jars, ashtrays, cigarette packs, pillow cases, plates, card holders, knives, mugs, jugs and every other conceivable china, brass or metal object.

In time, as with any other craze, the public tired of the verses. Kipling himself admitted he could cheerfully have killed the man who wrote them, had this not entailed committing suicide – and for a long time would not include the words among his collected Boer war verses, believing they had served their purpose and would be better forgotten.

The poem – with additional contributions from the proprietors of the *Daily Mail* – earned well over £340 000. "The Absent-minded Beggar" fund was utilised for anything from clothing wounded men to caring for their parrots; from building a

Caton Woodville lampoons his own creation in 1900, during the disillusionment of the war. But the verses had brought in showers of gold and silver (*right*) when sung by Lady Tree at the Palace Theatre.

model hospital with 300 beds to supplying thousands of tins of cocoa, bottles of wine and cases of soap. Free meals, transport, walking-sticks and deck chairs were among the items supplied to wounded soldiers. The fund even paid for fifteen marriage licences – after inducing the men to marry in the first place.

The critics were silenced at the song's staggering success, and by the money it raised. Kipling, refusing to accept remuneration, gave his original £250 fee from the *Daily Mail* to the fund; Sir Arthur Sullivan made a similar contribution of the £100 he received for setting the song to music.

In December 1899, Kipling was offered a knighthood which he declined, afraid that this public honour might endanger his independence. Carrie noted in her diary that, pleased as he was by the offer, Kipling felt he could "do his work better without it."

The war news from South Africa was cause for growing despondency. Before the first month was out, British civilians and soldiers were under siege in Mafeking, Kimberley and Ladysmith. Rhodes, who had travelled on the last train into the town, was pinned down in Kimberley. General Sir Redvers Buller, Commander-in-Chief of the British forces, suffered a disastrous defeat at Colenso, following unexpected and severe British losses at Stormberg and Magersfontein, in the bleak days of December known in Britain as "Black Week".

Though the war raged fiercely in the north, Cape Town was not threatened, and the Kiplings decided to spend the British winter at the Cape again. The popularity of "The Absent-minded Beggar" was still at its peak when they embarked in the *Kinfauns Castle* at Southampton on 20 January 1900. The war had fired national patriotism to an extraordinary degree, and the ship was filled with volunteers and nurses on their way to the front.

Reservations had been made for the Kiplings at Cape Town's best hotel, the Mount Nelson, which was already crowded with military staff, war correspondents, the members of various commissions, and the wives, mothers and sweethearts of British officers. The presence of refugee magnates from Kimberley and Johannesburg, plus camp followers and adventurers, had earned the hotel the nickname of "the Helot's Rest".

The Kipling family party was a source of interest to fellow guests. One of them reported in a letter home to England that Kipling was "a real good sort and absolutely regardless of his dress and appearance. The children . . . are nice little mites, quite young. He carries them about and wheels the perambulator about the grounds and sets all the ways of the high and mighty at defiance. He is an amusing talker and jokes frequently and often brilliantly. Here is absolute freedom from all side and affectation."[2]

Among the many war correspondents Kipling met at the Mount Nelson were H A Gwynne of Reuters and Perceval Landon of *The Times*, both of whom were to become close friends; Bennet Burleigh of the *Daily Telegraph*; Julian Ralph, an American representing the London *Daily Mail*; and L S Amery, formerly *The Times* correspondent in Pretoria, who was the Kiplings' table companion for several weeks.

The Mount Nelson Hotel in Cape Town provided a haven for wealthy refugees from the Transvaal during the Boer war, so that it was soon called "the Helot's Rest" – as portrayed in the bitter *Truth* cartoon of December 1900.

LE & TELEGRAPHIC ADDRESS.
"HOSTEL, CAPE TOWN."

Mount Nelson Hotel.
Cape Town. Feb 14 1900.

Dear Scully.

Thank you for your kindly little note and invitation. It's a tempting picture that you draw and I would we could come along and see you in your native heath but just now I'm dancing about among hospitals and running from one end of Capetown to the other trying to be of some use: and I don't know when I shall

Kipling stayed at the Mount Nelson in 1900. But his letter to writer WC Scully declines an invitation to socialise since he was too busy "dancing about among hospitals . . . trying to be of some use"

Kipling was given a pass to the war zone by Lord Roberts ("Bobs"), photographed *below* with his wife, one of his daughters, and his only son – who was killed in action at the very start of the Boer war.

A few days before Christmas 1899, in an attempt to turn the tide of military disasters, the British government had appointed Lord Roberts – at 67, England's greatest soldier – to succeed Buller as Commander-in-Chief in South Africa. On the afternoon his appointment was confirmed, he had been informed that his only son, Freddy, had been killed in action on 15 December during the battle of Colenso.

In Cape Town, the night before he left to take up his new command in the field, Roberts sent for Kipling and they spent the evening together; both men were in a grim mood over the recent revelations of Britain's unpreparedness for the war. Roberts, who was probably the first general to appreciate the importance of the press in wartime, arranged a pass to enable Kipling to go wherever he pleased. As the *Athenaeum* reported at the time, this may have been a kindness repaid: Kipling had, at Roberts' request, omitted the short poem "Bobs" from the volume of his collected verse. (It had first appeared in the *Pall Mall Magazine*, and Roberts appears to have found it objectionable not because of its title, but because of its inference that other generals indulged in "advertising".)

Kipling did not immediately put his pass to use. He spent several weeks visiting wounded Tommies in the army hospitals at Wynberg and Rondebosch, where they uncomplainingly suffered the effects of a wholesale shortage of medical personnel and supplies. Appalled to find a hospital so desperately in need of bandages in a city where there were plenty on sale, Kipling determined to contribute a load himself, only to be informed that army rules prevented the hospital authorities from receiving supplies from a private individual. "Well," said he, "I will dump the packages on the pavement before the door, and then tell them to come out and clear up the litter. They will get them into the building that way without tearing any red tape, I hope."[3]

Years afterwards, a Highlander who had spent some time in hospital in Rondebosch, recalled a chat with Kipling:

> "I had left my marquee to go out and sit under a tree and have a quiet cigarette when, on looking round, I saw advancing towards me a little man in a khaki serge suit, Eton jacket, black polished shoes and grey felt hat. He was looking for one of the Canadian sisters . . . He offered me a box of cigarettes and a copy of the *Army and Navy* . . . I believe he is gathering material for his book. He sees everything, I should imagine from his look and manner."[4]

In "Surgical and Medical", first published in May 1900, Kipling wrote with compassion about the wounded Tommies from "Home and all parts of the Empire", and of their hopes to settle in South Africa after the war. And in *Something of Myself* he remembered that he had been "persona gratissima" at certain Wynberg hospitals where the nurses found he was good for pyjamas. "Once I took a bale of them to the wrong nurse (the red capes confused me) and, knowing the matter to be urgent, loudly announced: 'Sister, I've got your pyjamas.' That one was neither grateful nor very polite."

In the north, Roberts was preparing to launch an offensive against the Boers, with his sights firmly set on the Free State capital of Bloemfontein. At Paardeberg

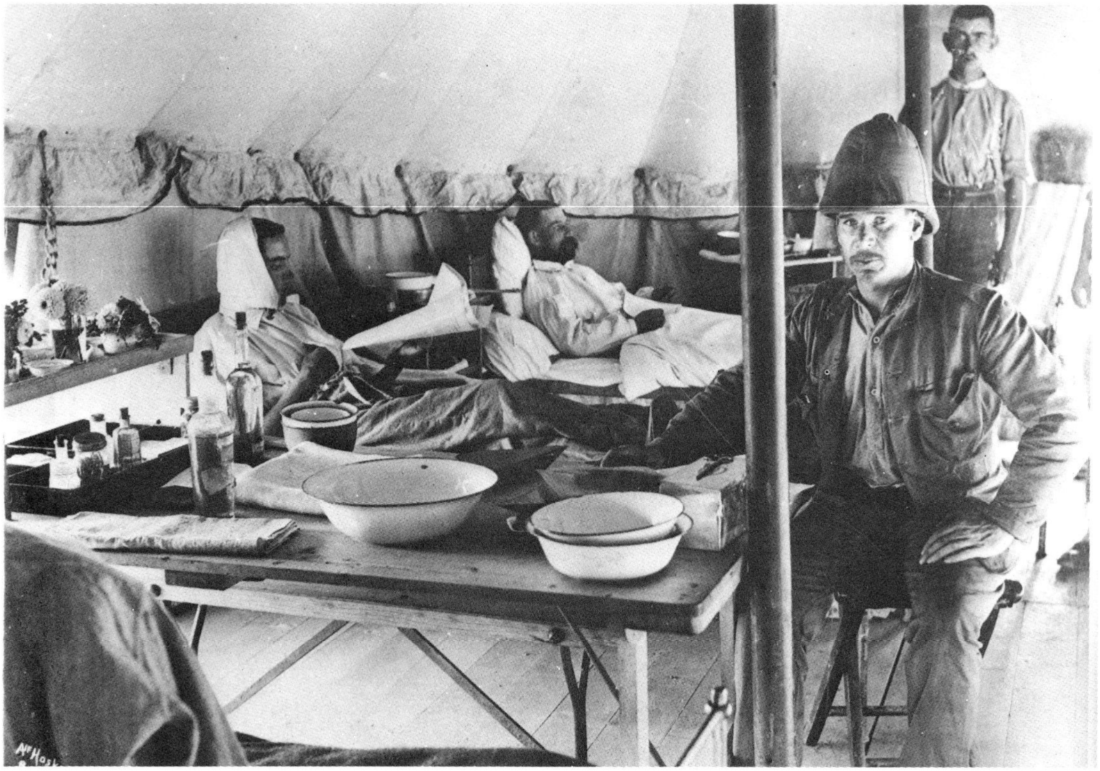

his troops engaged in ten days of fighting, before defeating the most formidable of the Boer leaders, General Piet Cronjé. By the time Cronjé surrendered, close on 1 300 British soldiers had been lost and a stream of wounded Tommies were arriving in Cape Town in hospital trains. Kipling set out to travel in one of the Red Cross ambulance trains to the rail-head at Modder River, and from there to make the return journey with the load of wounded. This was to be his first experience of war at close range.

Captain Llewellyn J. Phillips, commander of the Active Service Volunteer Company of the South Wales Borderers, travelled in the same carriage as Kipling to Beaufort West:

> "He was very affable (not at all the sort of fellow you would imagine from the description of him in the abortive attempts to get interviews with him) and seemed greatly interested in all the Volunteers in South Africa. When we got to Fraserburg Road, where the company of the Welsh are, he got out of the carriage, and was immediately surrounded by about fifty 'Tommies' and seemed in his glory in conversing with them. I never saw such hero-worship as at Beaufort West. It had leaked out that he was travelling by that train, and the whole of the town . . . crowded into the station to get a glimpse of him. This morning I received a packet containing two bottles of laudanum from him . . . I administered the first dose of it this morning and when I told the man from whom the medicine had come, his eyes gleamed with appreciation."[5]

Until Roberts' capture of Bloemfontein, Cape Town received all the wounded from the front: military hospitals were located in Rondebosch (*left*) and Wynberg. Kipling visited these men untiringly, arranging supplies of bandages, tobacco and magazines, and personally writing the letters dictated to him for those "at home".

Right: Kipling travelled on a hospital train after the Battle of Paardeberg; this is a letter he wrote on the return trip to Cape Town for Lance-corporal George Harris, who had lost his arm in the battle.

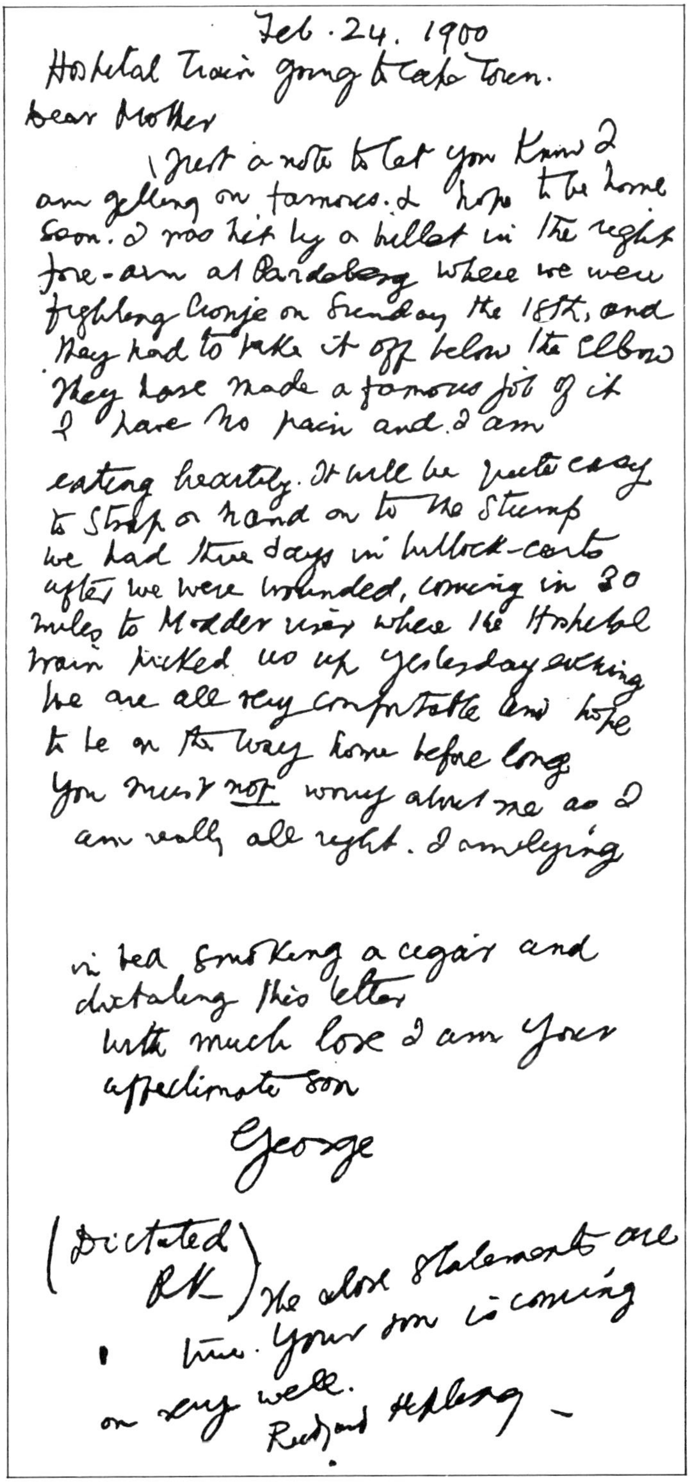

Feb. 24. 1900
Hospital Train going to Cape Town.
Dear Mother
I just a note to let you know I
am getting on famous. I hope to be home
soon. I was hit by a bullet in the right
fore-arm at Paardeberg where we were
fighting Cronje on Sunday the 18th, and
they had to take it off below the Elbow
They have made a famous job of it
I have no pain and I am
eating heartily. It will be quite easy
to strap a hand on to the stump
we had three days in bullock-carts
after we were wounded, coming in 30
miles to Modder river where the Hospital
train picked us up yesterday evening
we are all very comfortable and hope
to be on the way home before long
You must <u>not</u> worry about me as I
am really all right. I am lying
in bed smoking a cigar and
dictating this letter
With much love I am your
affectionate son
George

(Dictated
RK) The above statements are
true. Your son is coming
on very well.
Rudyard Kipling –

On the return journey to Cape Town, Kipling spent every available moment writing letters for those who wanted to send word to a wife or mother athome ("their first thought in every instance was that she should not worry"), and were unable to write for themselves. He signed his own name on them – an added bonus when his autograph was worth at least ten shillings at a time. Touched by the good-humoured courage as well as the suffering of the wounded men, he wrote movingly about his experiences in a sketch he called "With Number Three" (published in the *Daily Mail* on 21 April 1900):

> "The sun had faded the Red Cross on her panels almost to brick colour; had warped her woodwork and blistered her paint. For three months she had jackalled behind the army – now at Belmont, now at Magersfontein, now at Rensburg, and in that time had carried over thirteen hundred sick and wounded.
>
> In her appointments, her doctors, her two Nursing Sisters, and her nineteen orderlies there was neither veneer nor pretence, coquetry of uniforms, nor the suspicion of official side. She was starkly set for the work in hand, her gear worn smooth by use and habit, detailed for certain business only, and to that business most strictly attending.
>
> Since she started from no known platform I came aboard early, and while we lay silent as a ship in port, the big stock-pot purring in the kitchen, the bottles clicking in the pharmacy as the doctor counted them over, I felt that peace had never been in our generation – that Number Three Hospital Train – iodoform-scented, washed, scrubbed, and scoured – had plied since the beginning of time . . . We slipped out of Cape Town into the twilight at a steady twenty-five mile an hour on our six-hundred-mile journey North. Some day you in England will realise what it means to handle armies and their supplies over this distance on a single three-foot-six line . . . The setting of the picture hardly varied a hair's breadth. A single track, lifting and dancing in the heat, the brown, hairless hills dusted with split stones, the sleek mirages, the knots of khaki figures, the dingy tents, repeated themselves as though we were running in circles . . . Strictly in confidence, I may tell you that the Colonial Corps are riding just the least little bit in the world jealous. They have each the honour of a new country to uphold, and it is neck and neck between them. So I sat joyously on the rear platform while Number Three ran the links of Empire through my hands. English of the Midlands, Cockney, Scots, Irish, Welsh, Queenslander, Victorian and Canadian, one after another, we picked them up and dropped them with a flying word . . ."

Opposite: Lord Roberts receives the keys of Bloemfontein from the mayor. The surrender of the Free State capital marked the end of the conventional phase of the war; increasingly the Boers employed guerrilla tactics which successfully strung out the hostilities for a further two years.

4 Lessons of the war

Roberts entered Bloemfontein on 13 March 1900. Although the townspeople were hostile, he met no armed resistance. The next day he suppressed one of the town's two established newspapers, the Dutch-owned and virulently anti-British *Express*, and commandeered the other, the *Friend of the Free State*, owned by an Englishman who was pro-Boer. In their place he established a new paper, *The Friend*, probably the first professionally-produced army newspaper in military history, and offered the proprietor of the *Friend* £50 a week for the four to six weeks that he estimated his troops would be halted in Bloemfontein. He felt a newspaper of their own would bolster the morale of the Tommies now swarming about the town with very little to do.

Lord Stanley, Roberts' press censor, invited four war correspondents – Julian Ralph, Perceval Landon, H A Gwynne and F W Buxton of the Johannesburg *Star* – to act as editors of *The Friend*. Landon immediately requested a contribution from Kipling, and within 24 hours the paper had received his verses on the heroism of the Irish troops, in time for publication in the second issue on St. Patrick's Day.

THE FRIEND

BLOEMFONTEIN, WEDNESDAY, APRIL 4, 1900.

PROCLAMATION.

Proclamatie.

PROCLAMATION.

PROCLAMATION.

NOTICE.

PROCLAMATIE.

Kennisgeving.

NOTICE!

Proclamation.

Proclamatie.

Proclamation.

Proclamation.

KENNISGEVING!

Proclamatie.

Proclamatie.

J. LEVIN & Co.,
WHOLESALE MERCHANTS

VICHY-CELESTINS

LENNON LIMITED,

BARLOW BROS. & CO.

Oh! Terence dear, and did you hear
The news that's going round?
The Shamrock's Erin's badge by law,
Where'er her sons be found!
From Bobsfontein to Ballyhoek,
'Tis ordered by the Queen,
We've won our right in open fight,
The Wearing of the Green!

Front page of *The Friend*, 4 April 1900, during Roberts' occupation of Bloemfontein. Kipling was only too pleased to join the staff of the commandeered newspaper, to which he had already contributed St Patrick's Day verses (*above*). In the heady atmosphere of a wartime news office (*right*) are correspondents Gwynne (*far left*), Ralph and Landon, with an absorbed Kipling perched on the table correcting proofs.

The same day, 17 March, Lord Roberts wired a request to Kipling to join the staff of *The Friend.* Kipling accepted with alacrity. Before leaving Cape Town, he walked with Milner on the slopes of Table Mountain to discuss the newspaper's objective – how it should appeal to the Boer as well as to Briton, to help the former accept defeat and build a future under British rule.

In Bloemfontein the editors of *The Friend* had been eagerly awaiting Kipling's arrival, and for the next fortnight he was in his element. "We have put you down as an editor of The Friend, and we have announced it." Landon held his breath and waited. "Well," Kipling replied, "I should have been mortally offended if you had not. Where's the office? I want to go to work as soon as I have finished my grape jam."[1]

He threw himself with vigour into his work: proof-reading, setting the type himself whenever the compositor's work was too slow or too poor (possibly by design), and painstakingly reading every contribution from a Tommy. So many had sent in verses that Ralph declared the British army an "organised host of poets". Most of them emulated Kipling's own style, and although many of the verses were poorly written,

Kipling insisted they be printed unchanged; when one of the editors "improved" a Tommy's poem, he spent an hour putting it back into the original vernacular for publication.

With his pipe clenched characteristically between his teeth, Kipling worked with zest, introducing two new features ("Kopje Book Maxims" and "Fables for the Staff") which he wrote at top speed, without his usual revising and refining. In fact, Kipling happily contributed the copy for almost a third of the paper, filling in for the other editors who, as foreign correspondents, worked late into the night on their stories for London and Johannesburg. Kipling, happy to be at work in a newspaper office again, himself testified to the spirit of comradeship between the editors: "Heavens! How good it is to be with men who are doing things!" And, as a member of the team, he'd work away with enthusiasm: "Now, what shall I do? Write a poem, fill out cables or correct proofs?"[2]

The Friend was an enormous success. Lord Roberts demanded his copy hot off the press, and so many Tommies would crowd into the small office that Kipling often had to tell them: "Haven't any; go to Barlow's shop around the corner." The news-

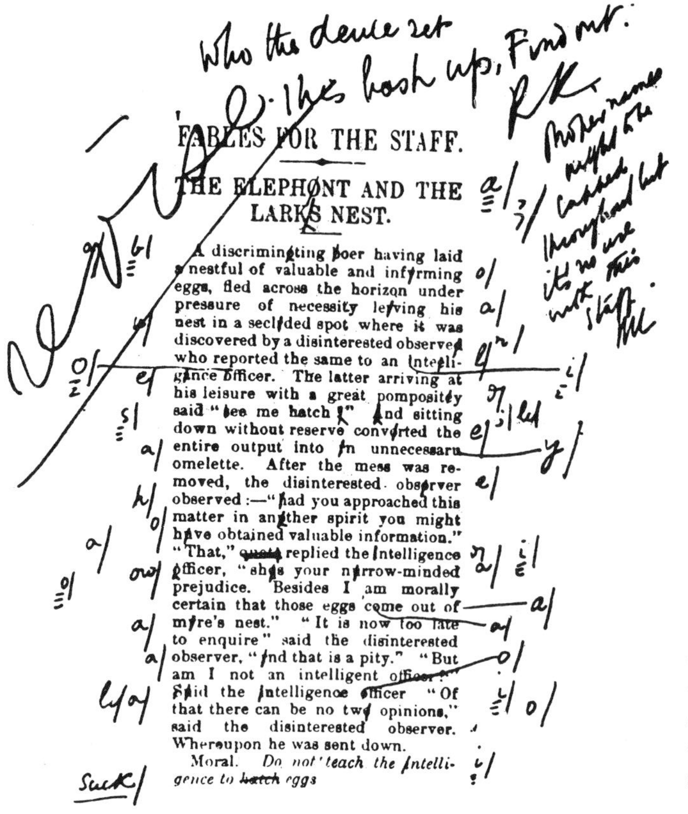

Who the deuce set this bosh up, Find out. RK

FABLES FOR THE STAFF.

THE ELEPHONT AND THE LARKS NEST.

A discriminating boer having laid a nestful of valuable and infyrming eggs, fled across the horizon under pressure of necessity leving his nest in a secluded spot where it was discovered by a disinterested observer who reported the same to an Intelligance officer. The latter arriving at his leisure with a great pomposity said "see me hatch it" and sitting down without reserve converted the entire output into an unnecessaru omelette. After the mess was removed, the disinterested observer observed :—"had you approached this matter in another spirit you might have obtained valuable information." "That," quoth replied the Intelligence officer, "shows your narrow-minded prejudice. Besides I am morally certain that those eggs came out of mare's nest." "It is now too late to enquire" said the disinterested observer, "and that is a pity." "But am I not an intelligent officer?" Said the Intelligence officer "Of that there can be no two opinions," said the disinterested observer. Whereupon he was sent down.

Moral. *Do not teach the Intelligence to hatch eggs*

Left: Kipling's exasperated comments on a proof of one of his "fables" for *The Friend:* "Who the deuce set this bosh up, Find out. RK". Dutch speaking compositors were suspected of sabotaging the staff's efforts.

Opposite: The cartoon of Kruger, by an unknown artist, expresses the jingoistic image of the Transvaal leader. In contrast, Boer general Piet Joubert (*far right*) was accorded great respect by his enemies.

paper was soon paying handsome profits. Previously the largest daily circulation of a Bloemfontein paper had been 400 copies. During its period of "war service", *The Friend* had a regular circulation of 5 000 to 5 500 copies, a tribute to its mixture of serious and light material.

In keeping with Kipling's original concept of reconciliation with the Boers, Commandant-General Piet Joubert's death evoked from him a generous valedictory tribute. Ralph noted that this was the only item of which the local compositors kept a copy.

With those that bred, with those that loosed the strife,
He had no part whose hands were clear of gain;
But, subtle, strong, and stubborn, gave his life
To a lost cause, and knew the gift was vain.

Later shall rise a People, sane and great,
Forged in strong fires, by equal war made one;
Telling old battles over without hate –
Not least his name shall pass from sire to son.

Sir Alfred Milner made a flying visit to Bloemfontein, and was a guest at a banquet at the railway station (which boasted the largest room in the town and the best cook in the Colony) given by the staff of *The Friend* in honour of Milner, Lord Roberts and Kipling. At the end of the evening, Kipling proposed a facetious toast to Paul

Kruger, "who has taught the British Empire its responsibilities, and the rest of the world its power, who has filled the seas with transports, and the earth with the tramp of armed men"[3] – a celebration of Jingoism in sharp contrast to the generosity of Kipling's recent tribute to a Boer general.

Roberts had at first believed that by capturing its capital he had come close to subjugating the Free State. However, the fall of Bloemfontein had prompted the Boers to find a new strategy in order to carry on the war against superior numbers and equipment. They gave up any attempt to confront the British forces head on, abandoned their cumbersome wagon trains, and concentrated instead on guerrilla tactics, forming their commandos into flying columns to strike behind the enemy lines.

This new phase of the war gave Kipling an opportunity to observe a military action at first hand. It was the only time in his life that Kipling, the soldier's poet, came under fire in the field. At the end of March, a force under General French was dispatched to secure an advance base at Karee Siding, 20 miles north of Bloemfontein, where it encountered a commando of Transvaal Boers. Though they outnumbered the Boers three to one, the British suffered the loss of 180 men before their fleet-footed enemy disengaged and withdrew to avoid being encircled by French's cavalry.

Kipling and Bennet Burleigh of the *Daily Telegraph*, escorted by a Guards officer, drove out of Bloemfontein to watch the battle in a Cape cart laden with food and drink for the party of journalists. There was, in fact, little to see:

> "The enormous pale landscape swallowed up seven thousand troops without a sign, along a front of seven miles . . . At last we came to a lone farm-house in a vale adorned with no less than five white flags. Beyond the ridge was a sputter of musketry and now and then the whoop of a field-piece. 'Here,' said my guide and guardian, 'we get out and walk. Our driver will wait for us at the farm-house.' But the driver loudly objected. 'No, sar. They shoot. They shoot me.' 'But they are white-flagged all over,' we said. 'Yess, sar. That *why*,' was his answer, and he pre-

War artist Mortimer Menpes' "Boer farmhouse" might have been sketched to illustrate the incident round which Kipling wove "A Sahib's War".

ferred to take his mules down into a decently remote donga and await our return. The farmhouse held two men and, I think, two women, who received us disinterestedly. We went on into a vacant world full of sunshine and distances, where now and again a single bullet sang to himself."

From their vantage point on the lip of a large hollow, Kipling and Burleigh came under sporadic rifle fire, "with a decent lull for meals", then the British artillery was brought into play and "for about two minutes a file of racing ponies, their tails and their riders' heads well down, showed and vanished northward". Twenty minutes of stronger bombardment from the British guns, and "a movement of men and horses from our side up the slope", signalled the end of the affray: "More Boer ponies on more skylines; a last flurry of pom-poms on the right and a little frieze of far-off meek-tailed ponies, already out of rifle range."

Kipling was to make use of the Boer farmhouse and the suggestion of treachery in a short story, "A Sahib's War", which he published in the following year.

Two days after the skirmish at Karee Siding, another British force under General Broadwood suffered a demoralising defeat at Sannah's Post, the site of Bloemfontein's water works.

Kipling had delayed his departure from Bloemfontein for a few days while he nursed Julian Ralph's fever-stricken son "with consummate skill and the gentleness of a woman".[4] His final contribution to *The Friend* was an appeal to the people of the Free State, composed with Ralph's assistance:

Soon after Kipling's return to the Cape, he was requested to write the lyrics for a special song to be sung by Florence Fraser, the "Free State Queen of Song", at a fund-raising concert in Bloemfontein. He telegraphed words to the tune of Auld Lang Syne, and the song took the house by storm, raising over £400. Florence Fraser described the event as "Something to remember for years, to remember with tears", and she kept the telegraph copy of the song until she died.

Kipling never included these light verses in any of his volumes, perhaps in deference to Lord Roberts who features in the rousing last verse:

And last to him, the little man who led our fighting line
From Kabul to Kandahar in the days of Auld Lang Syne.
For Auld Lang Syne, and Bobs, our chief of Auld Lang Syne,
We're here to do his work again as we did in Auld Lang Syne.

The British have come to stay.

Our students of political economy have taught us that the constitution and laws of the old Free State were as nearly perfect as any that could be framed for a democracy. The basis of the British Government is that of an enlightened and progressive democracy.

It is therefore certain that British rule will not bring any violent or revolutionary changes to the conditions under which you citizens have been living.

What are British principles?

The absolute independence of the individual, so long as he does not interfere with his neighbour's rights.

Prompt and equal justice, before the Lord, to all men.

A natural and rooted antipathy to anything savouring of military despotism, in any shape or form.

Absolute religious toleration and freedom of belief for all peoples.

Prompt and incorruptible justice to all men in every walk of life.

The right of every man to make his home his castle.

In view of these things and of the unalterable fact that the country has passed under a new rule, why should burghers hesitate or delay in making friends with the new situation?

Alert to every nuance of homesickness, Kipling immortalises an Australian soldier's experience of the Boer War. The verses became one of the popular "Service Songs" of the war:

Smells are surer than sounds or sights
To make your heart-strings crack

* * *

That must be why the big things pass
And the little things remain,
Like the smell of the wattle by Lichtenberg,
Riding in, in the rain.

We are your friends. We have never felt unfriendly towards you; for even in war we realised that you were deceived by unwise and selfish leaders.

Let us, then, repeat the new motto of the Free State, printed at the head of the newspaper, "All has come right," for we are certain that as soon as your people realise what is to be the new rule under which you are to live, you will know and acknowledge that the right has prevailed, and that never again shall you stand in fear of a military oligarchy like the Transvaal; or of tyranny or injustice in any form.

In a farewell editorial, Julian Ralph paid tribute to the talent Kipling had lavished upon *The Friend*, adding a personal accolade: "Great as our readers know him to be in literature, we know him to be even greater as a man."[5]

Kipling returned to Cape Town on the same train as Milner. He had revelled in the brief return to his old profession during his sixteen days of "active service". During his absence Carrie had enjoyed the company of an old friend, the West African traveller Mary Kingsley, who had volunteered to nurse Boer prisoners-of-war in a fever hospital in Simon's Town. She visited the Kiplings at the Mount Nelson Hotel shortly before they left the Cape for England; three months after they arrived home, the news reached them that she had died of typhoid early in June.

On their return to England late in April 1900, the Kiplings were welcomed back into the family circle at Rottingdean, and the children relished the summer picnics on the Downs with an assortment of cousins. But Rudyard, preoccupied with the war news from South Africa, was eager to involve himself with politics and the local war effort. In London he dined with the imperialist Colonial Secretary, Joseph Chamberlain; at home in Rottingdean he spent hours on the local rifle range, oversaw the building of a drill-hall, formed a volunteer company and a branch of the Navy League, and was chairman of all their managing committees.

On 15 March 1900 *The Times* had published "The Sin of Witchcraft", Kipling's fierce polemic demanding punitive action against those Cape colonists, both in and out of government office, who were actively or passively sympathetic to the Boer cause. His sentiments were endorsed in an editorial that declared:

> "Our loyal subjects and our troops have found themselves practically in an enemy's country. Mr Kipling draws for us a vivid picture of the governing gentlemen who have used their power in all sorts of quiet ways to make it felt everywhere that it does not pay to be loyal to the British flag . . . He appeals in the name of

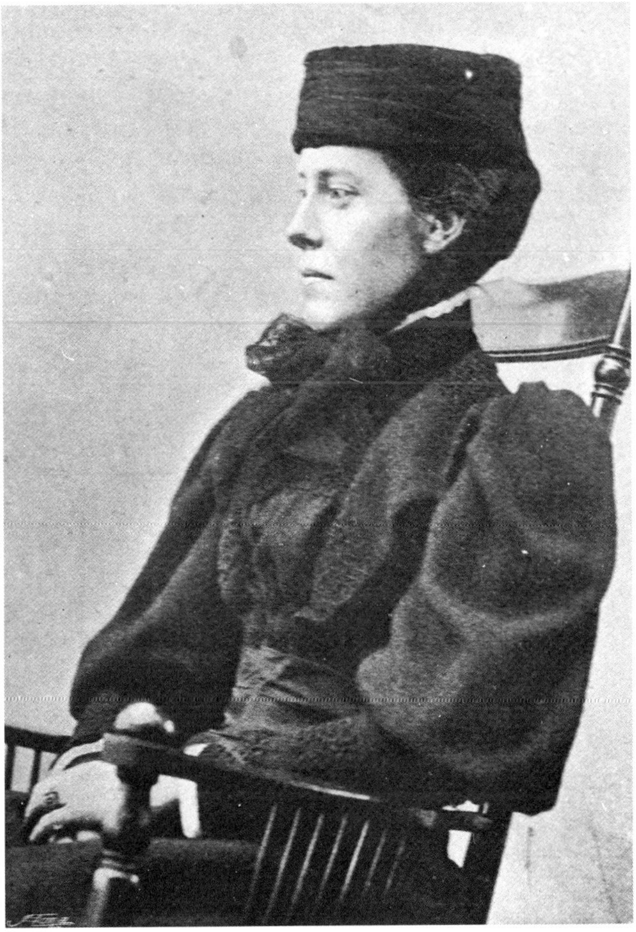

Mary Kingsley, intrepid British traveller and missionary in West Africa. Kipling, who had known her since his schooldays, admired her courage: "She must have been afraid of something, but one never found out what it was."

When the Anglo-Boer War broke out, she took a nursing course and sailed for the Cape. Here she was put to work at Simon's Town nursing Boer prisoners of war through enteric ("camp fever"). Appalled by "the stench, the washing, the enemas, the bedpans, the blood", and smoking cigarettes in a vain attempt to ward off the fever, she laboured day and night in charge of 100 men. Within two months she had succumbed to the fever. Her wish to be buried at sea was honoured: after a service in Simon's Town the coffin was taken out to sea beyond Cape Point.

the colony herself for such justice upon evildoers as shall reinstate her in the good opinion of the Empire."

Kipling's picture of overt and covert treachery would have been more vivid if he had not obscured its meaning with copious allegory. The anti-war (and anti-Kipling) periodical *Punch* commented:

To KIPLING, this: there are who much
Admire, they say, his rare and rich craft,
Yet marvelled at the double Dutch
That so obscured "The Sin of Witchcraft";
Who, having studiously toiled –
Opus inutile, infandum! –
Through all its paragraphs, were foiled,
And failed, they fear, to understand 'em.

. . . I rather think I can explain –
I'll clear up KIPLING's latest mud-yard.
I haven't studied quite in vain
The idiosyncracies of RUDYARD:
Benignant spectacles on nose
He's sailed six thousand miles of water
To howl in dull, confusing prose
For judgment, vengeance, blood and slaughter.

. . . Strange, is it not, so mild a man
Should want more blood when war is finished?
Should do the little best he can
Lest slaughter be perchance diminished?
Should deem debased beyond excuse
That statesman, cursed with wilful blindness,
Who bans the bullet and the noose,
And strives to do his work by kindness?

At the time of Victoria's Jubilee and the publication of "Recessional", three years earlier, Kipling had been a popular and uncontroversial figure, the "laureate of Empire". Now his Boer War writings were to make him a highly polemical one. Though he was still an influential writer with an enormous popular following, his imperialist vision came under increasingly bitter criticism from the anti-war faction in Britain and abroad. Though the mass of the British public remained unquestioningly loyal to the imperial cause, the Liberal opposition (and the newspapers that supported it) saw the Boer War as an expansionist attempt to break up a white nation and then rule it by compulsion. In their eyes, Kipling had become the "Bard of Bloodshed".

In addition to his polemical pamphlets, Kipling gave expression to his political

The rewards of fame: cartoons of Kipling abounded and were often ambiguous in intent.

views in fiction – the medium through which he could reach the widest audience – in four "Stories of the War" that appeared in serial form in the *Daily Express* between 12 June and 4 July. "The Way that he Took", "Folly Bridge", "The Outsider" and "A Burgher of the Free State" cannot be classed among Kipling's best work – as he himself recognised; only the first of them was republished, in a volume of short stories for scouts and guides (*Land and Sea Tales*, 1923).

His contemporary readers saw the pill beneath the fictional sugar-coating: the *Spectator* expressed the hope that the stories would bevery widely read "because they contain lessons of the war, moral and physical, theoretical and practical, which it is essential that the nation should learn if it is to become fit for its work."

The lessons were those that Kipling was often to repeat: Britain's military unpreparedness, and the inadequacy of a process of selection and training that sent into action officers who were bound by the rules and not the realities of war ("The Way that he Took", "Folly Bridge"), and were frequently incompetent snobs ("The Outsider"). "A Burgher of the Free State" drew for its setting on Kipling's brief experience of the Bloemfontein *Friend*; its eponymous hero is a newspaper compositor of Scots extraction, who is faced with a choice between his loyalty to the Free State and what Kipling interprets as a higher loyalty to British moral standards. The story is largely an attack on the Afrikaner Bond, "the curse of Africa . . . sowing seeds of dissen-

Kim, the Indian novel regarded by many as Kipling's finest work, began appearing in *Cassell's Magazine* in January 1901, while the Kiplings were summering at the Cape.

sion where none should exist", and a criticism of what Kipling saw as Britain's weakness towards her enemies, which she attempted to justify with the name of tolerance.

In the same summer of 1900, Kipling turned away from the issues of the Boer War to complete *Kim*, his farewell to India and his most successful full-length story; he had been working on it intermittently for more than seven years. *Kim* is remarkably free from the prejudice and bitterness which Kipling channelled into his writing about the Boer war, and exceptional in its tolerance and depth of understanding. Perhaps this was due to the influence of his father, whom he consulted closely throughout his writing of *Kim*.

In December 1900, with the English winter setting in, the Kiplings embarked for South Africa once again. On this voyage Kipling wrote "The Army of a Dream", a pamphlet in which he sketched his vision of the ideal English army, and called on Britain to secure its national defences by militarising every Briton from an early age.

The pamphlet was criticised as propaganda, but Kipling defended it as an attempt to save unnecessary losses on the battlefield by promoting military preparedness: "What I saw during the war of our arrangements and notions of work scared me, and I thought it might be good to train people before a real war came."

5 The deeper peace

When they landed at Cape Town on Christmas Day 1900, the Kiplings were met by Cecil Rhodes's carriage, and taken not to an hotel but to a house on the Groote Schuur estate that Rhodes had built and furnished for them: The Woolsack, which was to be their home for all the rest of their South African visits.

Rhodes had discussed the idea with the Kiplings when he returned to Cape Town in March 1900 after the 124-day siege of Kimberley. He was planning to build a small house on his estate that could be used by succeeding generations of writers and artists visiting South Africa; the young Herbert Baker, who had successfully remodelled Groote Schuur after its near-destruction by fire in 1896, was appointed as the architect. Carrie Kipling had accompanied Baker – who was to become a life-long friend – to choose the site. They found one close to Groote Schuur itself, separated only by a ravine filled with hydrangeas that became "one solid packed blue river" when the flowers bloomed. Rhodes took Kipling to see the site and asked him, "How would you like to hang your hat up there?"

Once the site had been selected, Rhodes wasted no time in getting the building started. It was designed in Baker's eclectic interpretation of the Cape Dutch style, a single storeyed white house with shutters and heavy doors of oiled teak. Intended primarily as a summer residence, it was built around an open atrium which created a tantalising inward view for the visitor arriving at the front door. Baker had been instructed by Rhodes "not to be mean", and to spare no expense in making the small house strong and beautiful. The Kiplings were delighted by the result: "A perfect Dutch house full of old Dutch things, with a long narrow garden in front and with Table Mountain rising out of our back yard. It's an enchanting spot, called Woolsack, because it has always been the highest seat on the mountain side." [1]

The Woolsack was Carrie's ideal house, her "dear Woolsack", and for four-year-old Elsie and three-year-old John it was paradise. There was a garden shaded with old oak trees, where cannas, arum lilies, roses, violets, fig and oleander, myrtle and plumbago flourished, and a hedge of banana trees afforded the children endless fun as they hunted – unsuccessfully – for an unsplit banana leaf. They had the excitement of encountering kangaroos, zebras, kudu, emus and a llama, all the beasts that roamed the Rhodes estate which was literally on their doorstep, while every morning they were woken by the roars of the lions in Rhodes's private zoo. Their alternative playground throughout the South African summer was the white beaches of Muizenberg, with their long lazy rollers and a treasure of shells for the finding.

It was during this first summer at The Woolsack that the Kiplings adopted a lion

Above: Kipling as dignitary, on board the *Kinfauns Castle* bound for Cape Town, December 1900.

Opposite: The Woolsack, the house which Rhodes had ordered to be built for the Kiplings, included a spacious panelled study (*top*) for the writer, and was planned round an open atrium (*below*) that was intended to give the occupants full enjoyment of the Cape's Mediterranean climate and light. (The house, designed by Herbert Baker, survives as part of the University of Cape Town; but the atrium has been covered over.)

cub, rescued by Rhodes's zoo-keeper when its mother tried to kill it. Carrie fed the cub with milk and water from a baby's bottle. Sullivan – a homely version of his Matabele name, Umslibaan – soon began to flourish, and was given the freedom of the house and garden. The children loved to watch him chase butterflies among the hydrangeas, "then lie down on the bare tiled stoop in the full glare of the sun, and you could step on him before you saw him; he would sit in the shadow of a wall or slide into a garden-border and till he moved you could not tell that he was there." [2]

For the adult Kiplings, The Woolsack provided the ideal setting: this was "the deeper peace of 'The Woolsack'", private enough for Rudyard to work without interruption or unwelcome visitors, yet easily reached by the friends they most wished to see. Rhodes was the most regular of their visitors, often in company with Dr Leander Starr Jameson, leader of the ill-starred Raid, who was now Member of the Legislative Assembly for Kimberley. In turn, the Kiplings dined frequently at Groote Schuur, which was open house for the people who would be most concerned in the remaking of South Africa once the war was finally over, including Milner's "kindergarten". A new friend was Major-General Robert Baden-Powell, hero of the Siege of Mafeking, who was later to found the Boy Scout Movement and who exchanged ideas with Kipling on the subject (it was one dear to Kipling's heart, in view of his belief in the need to train Britons for war from an early age).

Left: Rhodes looks on while the Misses Alexander warily admire a tiny lion cub from his private zoo at Groote Schuur. The cub was adopted as a pet by the Kipling family, and kept until it grew too big for comfort.

Opposite: Rudyard Kipling sketched from life by Major-general Robert Baden-Powell, photographed (*far right*) during the siege of Mafeking which guaranteed his fame. Baden-Powell shared Kipling's belief in the need to prepare youth for self-sufficiency in the field; he founded the Boy Scout Movement, for which Kipling was to write the "Patrol Song".

Although the major battles of the Boer war had been fought, the guerrilla phase dragged on over a wide front that extended down into the Cape Colony itself. The end appeared to be in sight: Lord Roberts had handed over his command to Kitchener, President Kruger had fled to Holland, and Milner had already been appointed civilian administrator of the not-yet-secured Boer republics. But on the Boer side the "bitter-enders" would not give up, and were supported by many of their fellow-Afrikaners in the Cape.

On the British side, Milner was determined that the war must be brought to a clean finish. There was to be total victory, not a patched-up peace that would permit the Afrikaner to preserve a separate political identity. The wearisome business of winding up the war was of less concern to most of Rhodes's visitors than the problem of how South Africa was to be governed after the peace.

Rhodes was aware that his health was failing (in fact, he had only another year to live), and that he would not realise his vision of a South Africa united under the British flag from the Cape to the Zambezi. He had turned instead to another dream: the creation of a new leadership elite, specifically selected and educated for the task, who would look to the peace of the world and combine to uphold it.

The cream of young Britons, British colonials, Americans and Germans were to be brought together and bound by a shared educational tradition, to emerge as future leaders of their different countries with a common aim and interest: the achievement of permanent world peace. To fulfil this aim, Rhodes intended to create a number of scholarships bearing his name, enabling 60 students from the British colonies,

100 Americans and 15 Germans (personally selected by the Kaiser) to read for their degrees at Rhodes's own alma mater, the university of Oxford.

Rhodes would often walk from Groote Schuur to The Woolsack to discuss his scholarship scheme over tea with Carrie Kipling, who was a firm favourite with him and probably the only woman with whom the great man was fully at ease. He valued her sensible advice and pungent observations, and recognised her talent for management that coped efficiently with all the practical arrangements of Kipling's life, freeing her celebrated husband for his creative work. Kipling himself was well aware of his dependence upon Carrie, and proud of her abilities, remarking, "If ever I had wanted to go off with someone else, Carrie would have had to arrange it for me and take our tickets."[3]

The work that Kipling had "managed to get through" during the South African summer of 1900–1901 included a polemical paper, "The Science of Rebellion", written for the Imperial South African Association and subsequently published in pamphlet form. Like "The Sin of Witchcraft", published in *The Times* a year earlier, this was an outspoken attack on the "disloyal" element in the Cape Colony. Kipling castigated both the Afrikaner Bond ("the right wing of the Republican armies"), for betraying Britain from within the Colony, and His Majesty's Opposition in Britain for advocating lenient treatment for the Cape rebels – "an invitation to loot and free-shooting". In a letter to his old Vermont friend, Dr James Conland, written at the same time (February 1901), Kipling expressed himself equally forcefully:

Rhodes in the midst of the YMCA Rambling Club on Groote Schuur. He was generous in allowing the public to roam his estate on the eastern slopes of Table Mountain. At his death, the estate was left to the nation, and the house to future prime ministers.

Our Sergeant-major's a subaltern ; our Captain's a Fusilier ;
Our Adjutant's "late of Somebody's 'Orse," and a Melbourne auctioneer ;
But you couldn't spot us at 'arf a mile from the crackest caval-ry—
They used to talk about Lancers once,
Hussars, Dragoons, an' Lancers once,
'Elmets, pistols, an' carbines once,
But now we are M. I. !
That is what we are known as—we are the orphans they blame
For beggin' the loan of an 'ead-stall an' fittin' a mount to the same :
'Can't even look at their 'orse-lines but someone starts bellerin' "Hi!
Hook it, you burglin' Ikona ! Foot-sack, you —— M. I. !"

We're trekkin' our twenty mile a day, an' bein' loved by the Dutch,
But we don't hold on by the mane no more, nor lose our stirrups—much.
An' we scout with a senior man in charge, where the 'oly white flags fly—
We used to think they were friendly once,
Didn't take any precautions once
(Once, my ducky, an' only once !),
But now we are M. I. !
That is what we are known as—we are the beggars that got
Three days "to learn equitation," an' six months o' bloomin' well trot !
Cow-guns, an' cattle, an' convoys—an' Mister de Wet on the fly—
We are the rollin' Ikonas, we are the —— M. I. !

Kipling's tribute to "M.I.", the long-suffering Mounted Infantry of the Boer war ("I wish my mother could see me now . . .") revealed the invariably sure grasp of local slang and army jargon that made his poems so popular with the troops.

"The Boers . . . are having the time of their lives – stealing from friends and foes alike and living on the fat of the land. . . . Cape Town is full of rebels and is the only place where martial law is not proclaimed. A man gets as much as 12 months imprisonment sometimes for assisting the enemy, and six months for helping to blow up a railway culvert. And then we wonder why the war doesn't end. They make no secret of their intentions. They want to sweep the English into the sea, to lick their own nigger and to govern South Africa with a gun instead of a ballot box. It is only the little Englanders in London who say that the Transvaal is merely fighting for its independence; but out here both sides realize it is a question of which race is to run the country."[4]

Rhodes was in England on business when the Kiplings' first summer at The Woolsack drew to an end in April 1901. Kipling wrote to announce their departure and to express their gratitude:

"We should be going off in the *Briton* on Wednesday and this is just to say goodbye for the present. The life in your 'cottage' has been as perfect in its peace and quiet as anything in this world could offer. It has filled me full of notions – over and above work that I have managed to get through – so that it will take me all my time to get them in order. I've done one or two things that I am rather pleased with but it has been horribly lonely since you left. Rather like living in a landscape with half the horizon knocked out.

Sullivan the Lion is at present in the pink of condition, so if anything happens to him after we go away it won't be our fault. He is, I believe, to be fed till he is too thick to slip between the bars of the big cages up the hill and then he is to take his place in society. He weighs about 12 pounds and is not quite safe with small children . . .

The wife is very sad at leaving the Woolsack, but finds consolation in leaving things behind for another year . . . We've been walking round the garden in the starlight and saying things about you that would look absurd on paper."[5]

(Sullivan the lion, in fact, did not long survive the Kiplings' departure; he died of colic soon after his removal to the less friendly environment of the Groote Schuur zoo.)

Although most of Kipling's Boer war verses did not appear for the first time until 1903, in a collected volume entitled *The Five Nations* (a description applied by Kipling to the British Empire – the Old Country, with Canada, Australia, South Africa and India), at least two poems were published in *The Times* half-way through 1901.

"Bridge-Guard in the Karroo" captures the splendour of a Karoo sunset and the loneliness of the vast African landscape, intensified by the brief appearance of the lighted north-bound train. It is a poem above the littleness of politics, but for the informed reader there is also an echo of Kipling's hospital-train article, "With Number Three". In that earlier work he commented on the little detachments of armed men who were set to guard the Cape railway line at "every bridge, every culvert, every point at which the line may be cut or blown up" by rebel colonists. "Bridge-Guard in the Karroo", with its repeated refrain (*No, not combatants – only/ Details guarding the line*) is a reminder of the unglamorous supporting roles that many must play in wartime, and a memorable evocation of the vast, lovely Karoo night.

"The Lesson", which appeared in *The Times* in July 1901, is not poetry but deliberately unpoetic, heavy verse, to drive its point home the more effectively. It reiterates the second theme that runs through all of Kipling's Boer war writing: Britain's military unpreparedness, her outdated and inefficient military system, which the war had shown up at enormous cost in lives and money:

It was our fault, and our very great fault, and
  not *the judgment of Heaven.*
We made an Army in our own image, on an island
  nine by seven,
Which faithfully mirrored its makers' ideals, equipment,
  and mental attitude –
And so we got our lesson: and we ought to accept it
  with gratitude.

We have spent two hundred million pounds to prove the
  fact once more,
That horses are quicker than men afoot, since two and
  two make four;
And horses have four legs, and men have two legs, and two
  into four goes twice,
And nothing over except our lesson – and very cheap at
  the price.

* * *

So the more we work and the less we talk the
  better results we shall get.
We have had an Imperial lesson. It may make us an
  Empire yet!

The Kiplings had already sailed from England to spend another summer at the Cape when a new long poem, "The Islanders", appeared in *The Times* of 4 January 1902, arousing a storm of protest. Kipling had brought the full power of his pen to bear in addressing the English people with what was at once a passionate castigation and a passionate appeal on the familiar subject of military preparedness. He warned that the English way of life – "the lordliest life on earth" – was not only worth defending, but would be doomed if England were not ready to defend it in the event of a major war. His appeal was for compulsory military service for all Englishmen:

Each man born in the Island broke to the matter of war.
Soberly and by custom taken and trained for the same;
Each man born in the Island entered at youth to the game. . .

Kipling lashed out at the pride and complacency that blinded the English to their own vulnerability, and at their refusal to give due attention to the arts of war; instead, they spent their energies on sport, making heroes of "the flannelled fools at the wicket or the muddied oafs at the goals".

Predictably, Kipling's attack on the sacred cow of English sport caused as great an outcry as his appeal for conscription, and angered his supporters as much as his enemies. The controversy had reached Cape Town by the time the *Kinfauns Castle*, with the Kipling entourage on board, docked on 7 January 1902. Among the newspaper reporters who besieged Kipling for a story was Edgar Wallace, whom Kipling had recommended to his old friend Harmsworth in London as a correspondent for the *Daily Mail*.

Settled in again at The Woolsack, Kipling turned his attention to completing the *Just So Stories* for children which he had been writing since 1897. Two of them have a southern African setting. "How the Leopard got his Spots" is set in the Transvaal highveld, while Kipling's visit to Rhodesia in 1898 produced "The Elephant's Child" – whose "satiable curtiosity" took him "from Graham's Town to Kimberley, and from Kimberley to Khama's Country, and from Khama's Country he went east by north, eating melons all the time, till at last he came to the banks ofthe great grey-green, greasy Limpopo River, all set about with fever trees."

Elsie Bambridge, Kipling's daughter, later recalled that the *Just So Stories* were

Left: On the long voyages to and from the Cape, Kipling often chose the company of children. These ones were fortunate in hearing the *Just So Stories* from the mouth of the author.

Right: Rhodes's seaside cottage at Muizenberg, photographed as it was when he spent the last days of his illness there in March 1902.

Below: Rhodes in rare relaxed mood and attire, playing chess with the ship's officer of the *Drummond Castle*.

Rhodes's coffin lies in state in the hall at Groote Schuur.

first read aloud to her and her brother John at The Woolsack, "for such suggestions as could be expected from small children. The illustrating of the stories gave their author immense pleasure, and he worked at them (mostly in Indian ink) with meticulous care and was delighted when we approved of the results."[6]

This time the pleasures of summer at The Woolsack were overshadowed for the Kiplings by alarm at the rapid deterioration of Rhodes's health. He had been warned by his doctor in London that, at 49, he had little longer to live; he had returned to Cape Town in January a sick man, and gone at once to his small seaside cottage at Muizenberg to escape the stifling summer heat. On 6 February Kipling heard that Rhodes was mortally ill, and from then on he visited him almost daily. Rhodes rallied enough in March to plan his return to England, but on the 18th he lost consciousness, and he died on the 26th – the day he was due to sail – reputedly murmuring "So little done – so much to do." That night his body was carried by moonlight to Groote Schuur, and laid out in a coffin of Rhodesian teak on a table in the wide hall.

A seemingly endless queue of people came to Groote Schuur to pay their last respects to Rhodes. Wreaths and cables arrived from all over the world, and in Cape Town businesses were closed and flags flew at half-mast. In Rhodes's will he had asked to be buried in Rhodesia, on a hill in the Matopos that he had named "View of the World". Jameson, as one of the executors, called Kipling into council to discuss the funeral arrangements.

Kitchener and Kipling as tin soldiers in *The Struwwelpeter Alphabet* of 1900.

Top: The Woolsack, the Cape home designed for the Kiplings by Rhodes's protégé Herbert Baker (*left*). The painting at Baker's feet shows the memorial he designed for Rhodes.

Above: Mortimer Menpes' impression of a relaxed Kipling in colonial field dress, during the Anglo-Boer War.

The rules of war and of that great British institution, cricket, were linked in colourful cartoons in the Christmas 1899 number of the pro-Liberal, anti-war magazine *Truth*. Blaming Joseph Chamberlain, as a "full-blooded, hot Imperialist", for the outbreak of the war, it proposed in verse a cricket match instead. The "United Universe Team" (*above*) was to include Kruger and the German kaiser, in gloves, as well as "the Brown man and the Black man and the Yellow man" . . . *Overleaf* are the "British Team" – Chamberlain with monocle and cigar, surrounded by the puppets of the cabinet – and "The Luncheon Break" – "when Society attends/to see all the foreign players and their polyglottic friends". Kipling, to the right beyond the portly Prince of Wales, is a distinctive figure in their midst.

Kipling too drew parallels between war and cricket, shocking Britain in 1902 by publishing "The Islanders", his stinging rebuke to a nation that had sent ill-prepared young men by the thousand to die in South Africa. *Overleaf* are selected lines from Kipling's long, intense tirade urging every Briton to be "entered at youth to the game – As it were almost cricket . . ."

Sons of the sheltered city – unmade, unhandled, unmeet –
Ye pushed them raw to the battle as ye picked them raw from
the street.
And what did ye look they should compass? Warcraft
learned in a breath,
Knowledge unto occasion at the first far view of Death?
So? And ye train your horses and the dogs ye feed and prize?
How are the beasts more worthy than the souls, your sacrifice?
But ye said, "Their valour shall show them"; but ye said,
"The end is close."
And ye sent them comfits and pictures to help them harry
your foes:
And ye vaunted your fathomless power, and ye flaunted
your iron pride,
Ere – ye fawned on the Younger Nations for the men who
could shoot and ride!
Then ye returned to your trinkets; then ye contented your souls
With the flannelled fools at the wicket or the muddied oafs
at the goals.
Given to strong delusion, wholly believing a lie,
Ye saw that the land lay fenceless, and ye let the months go by
Waiting some easy wonder, hoping some saving sign –

Idle – openly idle – in the lee of the forespent Line
Idle – except for your boasting – and what is your boasting
worth
If ye grudge a year of service to the lordliest life on earth?
Ancient, effortless, ordered, cycle on cycle set,
Life so long untroubled, that ye who inherit forget
It was not made with the mountains, it is not one with the
deep.
Men, not gods, devised it. Men, not gods, must keep.
Men, not children, servants, or kinsfolk called from afar,
But each man born in the Island broke to the matter of
war.
Soberly and by custom taken and trained for the same,
Each man born in the Island entered at youth to the
game –
As it were almost cricket, not to be mastered in haste,
But after trial and labour, by temperance, living chaste.
As it were almost cricket – as it were even your play,
Weighed and pondered and worshipped, and practised day and day.

"The Islanders"

Kipling may well have recalled wryly his 1898 ode to "Cricket", illustrated (*above*) by William Nicholson: "Thank God who made the British Isles,/And taught me how to play,/I do not worship crocodiles/Or bow the knee to clay!"

Left: The "muddied oafs at the goal" were joyfully depicted in this satirical French cartoon entitled "Football".

Opposite: Vanity Fair portrait of Dr Leander Starr Jameson, Kipling's closest friend at the Cape after Rhodes's death.

Overleaf: Kipling in William Nicholson's excellent sombre lithograph of 1904.

William Nicholson.

The funeral train that took Rhodes's body from Cape Town to Rhodesia, for burial in the granite-crowned Matopos hills.

On 2 April a short private service was held at Groote Schuur, and the coffin, draped in an old Union Jack that had hung in the billiard room, was taken under mounted escort to the Houses of Parliament in Cape Town to lie in state for a day and a night before the public service in the Anglican Cathedral. At the private ceremony, Kipling read the obituary verses he had written for his friend:

Dreamer devout, by vision led
Beyond our guess or reach,
The travail of his spirit bred
Cities in place of speech.

Always deeply affected by death, Kipling could not be persuaded to attend the burial in the Matopos. Rhodes's body was carried to Rhodesia in a funeral train draped in black and purple, and then placed on a gun-carriage drawn by twelve oxen. Thousands of Matabele tribesmen came to honour the dead man, and their royal salute – "Bayete!" – rang from hill to hill. Afterwards Jameson and Rhodes's brother Frank sent word to Kipling that his obituary verses had been read over the coffin as it was lowered into the grave.

Under the terms of Rhodes's will, all his immense fortune was placed in a trust fund, the bulk of it to be used for the public benefit. Groote Schuur, with its adjoining property, was left as an official residence for future prime ministers of a united South Africa. Kipling was to be allowed to retain the tenancy of The Woolsack for his lifetime – a right he never gave up, even after the family's visits to the Cape ceased altogether.

6 Half the horizon

Rhodes's funeral train had travelled through a country not yet formally at peace, but by now even the guerrilla war had almost run its course. In the second week of April 1902 – a few days before the Kiplings sailed from Cape Town to return to England, with Kipling's father and Jameson as fellow passengers – the delegates of the two Boer governments held their first meeting with Kitchener in Pretoria to arrange the terms of surrender.

On 31 May 1902 the Treaty of Vereeniging was signed and the Anglo-Boer War was finally at an end. The two Boer republics were to submit to the authority of the British crown, but it was agreed that a unified South Africa was to be granted self-government "as soon as circumstances permit". The important question of the black franchise was to be left in abeyance until after the grant of self-government. Cape rebel leaders were to be tried by court-martial, and the rank and file disfranchised (though in the event this was for five years only). The Dutch language would be admitted in the law courts, and could be taught in schools where parents so wished.

These were not the terms that the imperialists had hoped for, in order to anglicise the new South Africa. No target date had been set for self-government, but it was clear that Milner and his "kindergarten", his picked and youthful administrative staff, would have limited – and probably insufficient – time to rebuild the old republics on British lines before they were handed back to their Boer rulers.

England first read the news of the peace in the *Daily Mail* of 1 June – a "scoop" for Edgar Wallace. The next day was celebrated as a public holiday, but not everyone welcomed the defeat of the Afrikaner nation, or was convinced of the justice of the British cause. In Rottingdean, Kipling's Aunt Georgie Burne-Jones declared that a day of mourning was called for, and hung a black banner from a window of North End House, inscribed with the words, "We have killed and also taken possession." By evening a crowd of young men from the village had gathered and almost set the hedge alight in their attempts to pull down the banner. Kipling hastened to Aunt Georgie's rescue and persuaded the demonstrators to depart.

The incident was of little consequence in itself, but it angered Kipling enough to make him close the rifle club he had initiated, and it confirmed his and Carrie's decision to leave Rottingdean, a move they had been considering for some time. Fortunately, they had found the house they had been looking for, "a real House in which to settle down for keeps": Bateman's, a square stone-built Jacobean house at Burwash with 33 acres of land.

The move to Bateman's – the last the Kiplings were to make – took place at the beginning of September. Kipling discovered and rejoiced in the timeless traditions

Kipling's Aunt Georgie, Lady Burne-Jones, was a Boer sympathiser. She hung a black banner from her window when peace was declared.

of the English countryside. With his usual pleasure in mechanical things, he set about harnessing the mill-stream at the bottom of the garden to provide electricity for the house. As the work went on, he developed a deep respect for the Sussex countrymen whose skills were rooted in tradition – "artists and craftsmen, either in stone or timber, or wood-cutting, or drain laying or – which is a gift – the aesthetic disposition of dirt."

But even the Kiplings' happiness in Bateman's could not fend off the rigours of the English winter, and again they made the annual voyage to Cape Town for the warmth of the southern summer. The return to The Woolsack was as joyful as ever:

> ". . . the friendly, well-known Mountain and the rush to the garden to see what had happened in our absence; the flying barefoot visit to the neighbours the Strubens at Strubenheim, where the children were regularly and lovingly spoiled; the large smile of the Malay laundress, and the easy pick-up-again of existence."

For Kipling, however, Rhodes's absence cast a constant shadow. He unburdened his feelings in a letter to Dr Conland:

> "I had intended to do several things, including a trip up country . . . but Mr Rhodes' death has changed all that. No one could give you any idea of that great spirit's power or the extent to which the country worshipped him. His funeral was the most marvellous thing I have ever seen – a whole city of 60 000 moved as one man with a common grief and reverence. It seems absurd to speak of my own petty loss in the face of this great public calamity, but I feel as though half the horizon of my life had dropped away. He was always a close friend of mine – and there was so much to do."[1]

Kipling in sociable mood at a Cape garden party in 1903, probably during the tour of the Colonial Secretary, Joseph Chamberlain, after the Anglo-Boer War. Kipling confessed that summers at the Cape were his "political" time – "and I enjoy it." It was at Bateman's, in England, that his writing took precedence.

Jameson's imperialist Progressive Party was still active in opposing the strongly-supported Afrikaner Bond. The summer before, Kipling had spoken in support of the Progressives at a Cape Town political meeting, and he had attended several other such meetings over the years. Now he was invited to contest a Cape constituency for the Progressives in the forthcoming general election. He declined the invitation. Although he admitted, "My half year at the Cape is always my 'political' time and I enjoy it,"[2] Kipling would not commit himself to formal allegiance to any party either in South Africa or at home.

Kipling's involvement with South African politics and politicians is reflected in much of what he wrote about the country, often to the detriment of his writing. His post-war poem of reconciliation, "The Settler", was published in*The Times* in February 1903:

Here, in a large and a sunlit land,
Where no wrong bites to the bone,
I will lay my hand in my neighbour's hand,
And together we will atone
For the set folly and the red breach
And the black waste of it all;
Giving and taking counsel each
Over the cattle-kraal.

It is a graceful epilogue from the "laureate of Empire", but it carried hope rather than conviction that the new South Africa would forget the past and work for a united future. The poem is the peacemaking gesture of a good winner, generous in victory. Its message was a welcome one to a country tired of war, and with a divided conscience about the justice of the cause it had been fighting for; it was received with enthusiasm in South Africa, where an anonymous Dutch version, "Verzoeningslied", appeared in a newspaper soon afterwards.

In contrast, a poem written at about the same time, "Dirge of Dead Sisters", is a moving and personal tribute to the dedication and sacrifice of Kipling's old friend Mary Kingsley and her fellow nurses. Here is Kipling the artist responding from the heart to what he has seen and felt, rather than Kipling the political thinker with a lesson to impart:

Who recalls the midnight by the bridge's wrecked abutment
(Autumn rain that rattled like a Maxim on the tin ?)
And the lightning-dazzled levels and the streaming,
straining wagons,
And the faces of the Sisters as they bore the wounded in?

* * *

Who recalls the noontide and the funerals through the market
(Blanket-hidden bodies, flagless, followed by the flies?)
And the footsore firing-party, and the dust and stench and
staleness,
And the faces of the Sisters and the glory in their eyes?

Both "The Settler" and "Dirge of Dead Sisters" were among the South African poems published in the collected volume, *The Five Nations*, in 1903. Besides the earlier verses, fifteen poems – most of them making their first appearance in print – and a dedicatory verse were included in a seperate section under the title "Service Songs". These were dedicated to "The Service Man" –

Batt'ry, brigade, flank, centre, van,
Defaulter, Army corps –

Kipling, as always, was quick to express his admiration of the common soldier, "lacking in everything but courage". Much of "Service Songs" is barrack-room balladry – tributes to the various branches of the armed services – but the first of the verses, "Chant-Pagan", breaks new ground in its voicing of political and social awareness on the part of the returned soldier:

Me that 'ave been what I've been,
Me that 'ave gone where I've gone,
Me that 'ave seen what I've seen –
'Ow can I ever take on
With awful old England again,
An' 'ouses both sides of the street,
And 'edges two sides of the lane,
And the parson an' 'gentry' between,
An' touchin' my 'at when we meet –
Me that 'ave been what I've been?

"The Lesson" and "The Islanders" were both reprinted in *The Five Nations*, together with a very different poem with the same theme: Kipling's preoccupation with the state of England's defences. "The Dykes", with its extended sea-imagery, is a parable dealing with the fate of those who have forgotten how to hold the land from the sea of the toil of their fathers. But, unlike the two earlier poems that sought desperately to goad Britain into action, the tone of "The Dykes" is not provocative, registering instead a profound sense of failure.

"The Pen mightier than the Sword" – this American cartoon depicting Kipling's rout of John Bull, appeared after the poem "The Islanders" had shaken his public with its trenchant criticism of British customs.

Three Boer War stories, "A Sahibs' War" (which appeared in the *Windsor Magazine* at the end of 1901) as well as "The Comprehension of Private Copper" and "The Captive" (both of which were published for the first time in 1902), were collected in Kipling's 1904 volume of short stories, *Traffics and Discoveries*. The messages they carry – the pills beneath the jam of Kipling's story-telling art – are less simple and less obvious than those of the earlier "Stories of the War", but they are present nonetheless.

Kipling's supreme gift was the ability to get inside the skin of his characters so that they speak with their own voices, but in these stories the characters are mouthpieces for their author's views – Kipling is on the outside, doing the talking himself. His familiar criticism of the British army for the shortsightedness and hidebound attitude of its senior officers, and the lack of training for its men before they were sent into the field, is expressed yet again – through the Sikh spokesman of "A Sahibs' War" ("new Sahibs from God knows where, who had never seen a tent pitched or a peg driven. They were full of zeal, but empty of all knowledge"), and through the Boer general of "The Captive" ("you send to England and make us a present of two – three – six hundred young men, with rifles and wagons and rum and tobacco").

It is Kipling himself, rather than the British general in "The Captive", who can be heard describing the Boer War as "a first-class dress-parade for Armageddon" –

Indian grooms round a campfire during the Anglo-Boer War. Many regiments had come straight from India, complete with Sikh batmen and grooms; the narrator of "A Sahib's War" (one of Kipling's more successful Boer War stories) is a Sikh. They were, of course, not permitted to bear arms in a "white man's war".

the major war for which, when it came, he was afraid Britain would find herself unprepared.

"The Comprehension of Private Copper" and "A Sahibs' War" are both about betrayal. In "A Sahibs' War", a young British officer is trapped and killed because he trusts a Boer family's false oaths of loyalty. The story might have been titled "The Comprehension of Umr Singh", because it is the young officer's Sikh servant who recognises, although the British officers do not, that the Boer enemy will not honour the unwritten rules of a gentleman's war.

The traitor in "Private Copper" is Britain herself; the Transvaal burgher who takes Copper prisoner (and is then captured in turn) is the son of an Englishman "betrayed by England" when the Transvaal was handed back to the Boers after Majuba, breaking Wolseley's promise that it would remain forever under English rule. The story suggests that with no support from England, and no acceptance by the Boers, the Uitlanders in the Transvaal were stripped of all self-respect. No longer British, but not Boer either, Copper's captor has become a degraded creature, a half-caste in everything but blood.

Although the poetry Kipling wrote about South Africa, or in response to the South African situation, reaches greatness on occasion, none of his South African prose can be counted among his best work. His contemporaries recognised that politics and literature made dangerous bedfellows. When "The Settler" had first appeared in print after being cabled to *The Times*, the critic of a rival newspaper dubbed Kipling "the poet in the telegraph office", warning that "you cannot, if you are an artist, play with the material of politics without suffering some damage from

Left: Barbed wire fences off the bathing beach for Boer prisoners of war at Simon's Town. Kipling's story "The Captive" opens with a description of their "shrimp-pink bodies" in the green water.

Right: Stephen Black, the young *Cape Argus* journalist whom Kipling encouraged to "discover South Africa as I discovered India". Black became a successful playwright, and treasured his impressions of Kipling, including some of his maxims for young writers: "Read the Bible"; "Never think of money when you write"; "What is true for Cape Town is true for everywhere"; "Don't trouble about plots or involved stories – describe" (*Strange Africana Library*).

contact with stuff so foreign to your element . . . Art must be worked at, and so must politics; and the man who works at the one and plays with the other is apt to excel in neither."

Kipling himself admitted to his young journalist protégé Stephen Black that he had failed to make literature out of South Africa, though it was his view that a man could not write anything of value about a country unless he had been born there. His love for the land itself was real and apparent; his moments of true poetry were almost always inspired by his response to the beauty of the South African landscape. But what is missing is any sense of continuity with the past, that magical dimension that underlies Kipling's writing about England and India. His vision of England was of a peopled countryside, with roots going back to the beginning of time; in India, he recognised and respected an ancient tradition without needing to understand it. But he failed to see South Africa as a country with a history.

Kipling's vision of South Africa was limited by a deep conviction that the best, perhaps the only hope for its future lay in colonising it with British settlers, "*picked* men . . . and breeding women", who would bring with them their own traditions. He did not have sufficient understanding of or sympathy for either its Boer or its black inhabitants, nor for their past, to be able to draw inspiration from the country.

The most fully-drawn of Kipling's South African characters, the "Burgher of the Free State", is a Scot, not an Afrikaner, and epitomises the Scots virtues. Even "Piet", the tribute to a brave enemy that Kipling included among the "Service Songs" in *The Five Nations*, contains a sting in the tail – a charge of rapacity – to detract from the Boer's claim to respect.

SOUTH AFRICAN ROYAL MAIL SERVICE

MENU

R.M.S. "KILDONAN CASTLE."

HOT

Consomme en Tasse

Plain and Devilled Whitebait

Golden Buck

COLD

Salmon Mayonnaise — Sardines

Chicken en Belle Vue

York Ham a la Gelee — Foie Gras en Aspic

Chaudfroid of Lamb Cutlets

Devilled Ham Toast

Salade a l'Espagnole — Sandwiches Assorted

Cherry and Genoa Cake

Vanilla Cream — Curacoa Jelly — Fancy Pastry

Petits Fours

Strawberry and Neapolitan Ices

Dessert — Cheese Assorted — Coffee

FANCY DRESS BALL SUPPER, THURSDAY, JANUARY 8TH, 1903.

The Union-Castle Mail Steamship Co Ltd

Donald Currie & Co, Managers, 3 & 4, Fenchurch St London, E.C.

The sea voyages to and from the Cape, escaping the English winter to enjoy a doubled summer season each year, continued to be a regular part of the Kiplings' lives until 1908. They usually embarked at Southampton just before Christmas, with two maids and a governess in attendance, surrounded by large black-domed trunks and boxes of books. After unpacking, the children would go off at once to see if any of their favourites among the stewards and crew of the Union-Castle Line were on board. Kipling always declined to sit at the captain's table; the family preferred to have a small table in the dining saloon to themselves, and "the first on the port side" was regularly reserved for them.

Kipling invariably worked during the voyage, either in his small cabin opening on to the promenade deck or at a folding table on the deck itself. Oblivious to the activity around him, he would pace about or busy himself at his writing pad as if he were working in his study at home. He seemed quite unconscious of the interest his presence sparked among his fellow-passengers. There were often friends on board: Jameson, Baden-Powell, the gold magnate Abe Bailey, and other men involved with South African affairs at that time, with whom Kipling shared long talks and immeasurable deck-pacing. He commented that "ship-board life going and coming was a mere prolongation of South Africa and its interest".

Summers at The Woolsack continued to follow the easy established pattern, with the children spending much of their time on the beach at Muizenberg. Even Kipling regarded this as a holiday time, claiming that he worked three times harder in England than he did at the Cape. An enthusiastic motorist, he was an early member of the Royal Automobile Club at the Cape, and he spent time browsing in Cape Town's junk shops and book stores – at times ranting wildly when he found his own works unavailable in the city.

Kipling was still a regular visitor to the offices of the *Cape Times*, enjoying sustained contact with the world of newspapers. Maitland Park, the sub-editor on the Allahabad *Pioneer* who had mercilessly corrected his copy and whose discipline he well remembered, had been appointed editor of the *Cape Times* in 1902 on Kipling's recommendation. Their friendship deepened in these years, during which Park vin-

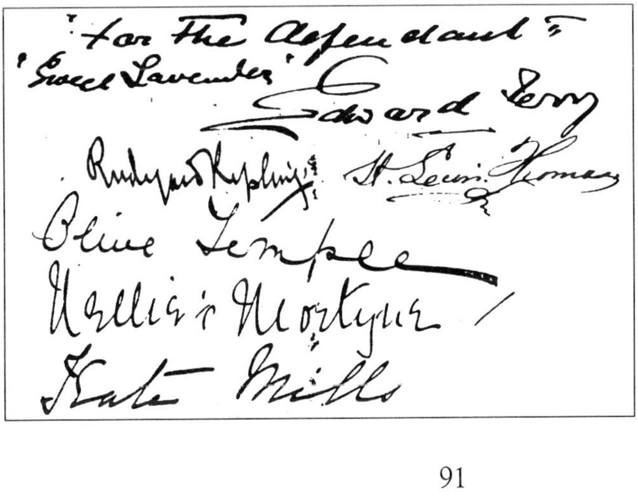

The sea voyages between England and the Cape were a prominent feature of the Kiplings' lives for the nine years they travelled on the mail-ships. The voyage took about 17 days, a leisurely, well-fed time filled with entertainments. Kipling was an honoured guest and personal friend of Union Castle chief, Sir Donald Currie

dicated Kipling's confidence to the full. An excellent editor, Park silenced all critics with the speed and thoroughness of his assimilation of the South African scene.

In 1904 Jameson's Progressive Party was returned to power in the first post-war election, largely due to the disenfranchisement of the Cape rebels. With the threat of Afrikaner Bond supremacy in the Cape countered for the time being, Jameson moved into Groote Schuur, which Rhodes had bequeathed to the nation as the official residence of the Prime Minister. Here Jameson extended the old hospitality to the Kiplings, and to the circle they shared.

Kipling, a self-professed admirer of Jameson's "infinite patience and statesmanship"[3], pinned most of his hope for South Africa's future on the man he saw as Rhodes's natural heir and successor. As he had written to Maitland Park, "He represents Rhodes and Rhodes was Africa."[4] Kipling's admiration for Jameson, like his admiration for Rhodes, was based on far more than political considerations; in

Opposite page: The summer months at the Cape were a seemingly endless holiday for the Kipling children. Here Elsie and John are photographed sandwiched between the Bailey children on the beach at Muizenberg, where they spent so many hours.

Kipling took an active interest in Cape politics and newspapers, including the appointment of Maitland Park as editor of the influential *Cape Times* in 1902. He had worked with Park in India, as recalled (*right*) by Cape cartoonist DC Boonzaier.

After Rhodes's death, Kipling's closest friend at the Cape was Dr Jameson (*below left*), Rhodes's erstwhile protégé who was now, as premier of the Cape, Kipling's neighbour at Groote Schuur.

Famous actress and beauty Lillie Langtry (*below right*) visited Groote Schuur while touring South Africa in 1906. Kipling accompanied the "Jersey Lily" on a brief Table Mountain ramble.

The Rhodes Memorial, situated higher on the mountain than his former home Groote Schuur, commands an imposing view that was Rhodes's favourite at the Cape. The official opening (*above*) was held in 1912, with Earl Grey officiating. The design, in which Kipling had played his part, was a shrine of Table Mountain granite designed in the style of a Greek temple by Herbert Baker; it contained a quotation from Kipling beneath a bust of Rhodes by JM Swan (*see page* 96), here still awaiting its unveiling. Bronze lions, also by Swan, line the sweeping steps. The impressive statue "Physical Energy" dominates both foreground and outlook (*see opposite page*). GF Watts is shown working on the statue in Philip Burne-Jones's painting (*right*); it was originally intended for a memorial in the Matopos, but the difficulties of transporting the statue across southern Africa lead to its inclusion in the Cape memorial. Kipling told Baker he had gone to the memorial by moonlight and found it "a thing to rejoice and sing over".

Something of Myself he confessed that the famous poem "If-" was "drawn from Jameson's character". (The verses were written in 1909 – 1910, after one of Jameson's visits to Bateman's and when he was no longer Prime Minister of the Cape.)

Kipling still had Rhodes much in his mind at this time, and he spent many hours actively helping to plan the proposed memorial to the great man. Herbert Baker had been the obvious choice as architect, and a site had finally been chosen on the slopes of Table Mountain among the silver trees and pines, with views of both sides of the peninsula. The dramatic focal point of the monument was to be Watts' equestrian statue "Physical Energy", originally designed to commemorate an ancestor of the Duke of Westminster. To Watts, the horse reined in from a full gallop, with its rider scanning the distance, was "an emblem of energy and outlook" that had been characteristic of Rhodes.

Kipling undertook to provide the inscription for the memorial, and chose to use

the last four lines from his obituary poem, in the hope that "those who go up to the memorial may come down from the mountain with perhaps more strength and belief. That is what mountains and memorials are for"[5]:

The immense and brooding spirit still
Shall quicken and control.
Living he was the land and dead
His soul shall be her soul.

7 A dream ends

Long before Rhodes's memorial was completed, Lord Milner, whom Kipling had believed would make "a sane and orderly success" of the reparation programme in South Africa, was recalled to London at the end of his term of service in 1905. His intention had been to encourage British emigration to South Africa, and to lay the groundwork for progressive policies in the country in anticipation of the granting of self-government to the former Boer republics. This design would take time to effect; self-government would have to be postponed until land settlement and administrative reform were well under way.

But shortly after Milner's return to England, a new Liberal government was returned to power with an overwhelming majority, and the Conservative policies

Milner in thoughtful mood as he sails home to England on leave during the Anglo-Boer War. He had been working in South Africa with his "kindergarten" – Merriman's term for the group of gifted young men, including Patrick Duucan and John Buchan, whom he had gathered about him to plan the reconstruction of South Africa after the war. Recalled to Britain in 1905, Milner came under criticism in a changed political climate – yet another disappointment for Kipling in the aftermath of the war.

affecting South Africa were reversed. Milner came under harsh criticism and retired into private life. In June 1907 full self-government was granted both to the Transvaal, where Louis Botha was elected Prime Minister, and to the renamed Orange River Colony under the leadership of Abraham Fischer. The Cape Colony election of 1908, held after the re-enfranchisement of the Cape rebels, brought a further blow for the imperialists: the Progressives were defeated by the South African Party, led by J X Merriman, which had the support of the Afrikaner Bond.

Kipling paid his tribute to Milner, and voiced his indignation at the treatment he had received, in "The Proconsuls":

They that dig foundations deep,
Fit for realms to rise upon,
Little honour do they reap
Of their generation.

Like many other Conservatives, Kipling felt that the Boer War had been fought in vain; Britain's victory had been shown to be hollow. His dream of a South Africa with a British future was shattered.

But Kipling's disillusionment was softened by a new romantic vision of England's past. The deep sense of the continuity of English history and tradition that he had discovered while living at Bateman's found expression in two volumes of linked stories, *Puck of Pook's Hill* and *Rewards and Fairies*, published in 1906 and 1910. Much of the writing of these stories was done at The Woolsack, and much of the research in the South African Library in Cape Town.

See you our little mill that clacks,
So busy by the brook?
She has ground her corn and paid her tax
Ever since Domesday Book.

* * *

Trackway and Camp and City lost,
Salt Marsh where now is corn;
Old Wars, old Peace, old Arts that cease,
And so was England born!

The summer of 1908 was the last that the Kipling family were to spend at the Cape. The children were growing older and the annual three months' holiday away from home was beginning to present practical difficulties. Rhodes was dead; Milner had left South Africa; Jameson would soon return to live in England. The old easy intercourse with Groote Schuur was over. As Kipling saw it, "the handing over of a higher civilisation to a lower is a heart-breaking job".[1] He did not want to be present to watch it in progress.

Later that year, a National Convention was called to draw up a new constitution for a unified South Africa. The draft South Africa Bill was taken to London in mid-

The Kipling family – Carrie, John, Rudyard and Elsie – photographed during their last South African summer, in 1908. John was to join the Irish Guards in 1914, and died at the Battle of Loos in 1915.

1909, and on 28 June the *Morning Post* published Kipling's long poem "The City of Brass", a bitter outpouring of his disgust and sense of betrayal. So far from benefitting from the "imperial lesson" of the Boer War, he believed that the British were plunging feverishly upon their own destruction, as

They unwound and flung from them with rage,
as a rag that defiled them,
The imperial gains of the age which their
forefathers piled them.

Kipling expressed his opinion of the new Union of South Africa rather more prosaically in a private letter in the following year, after the South Africa Act had received royal approval:

> "I suppose the Union is a great and joyous Fact. All I can see at this distance, with the naked eye, is the strongest purely Dutch Government that has ever succeeded to the throne of the entire sub-continent . . . (and) that the Dutch are scientifically turfing out the English in favour of their own interests."[2]

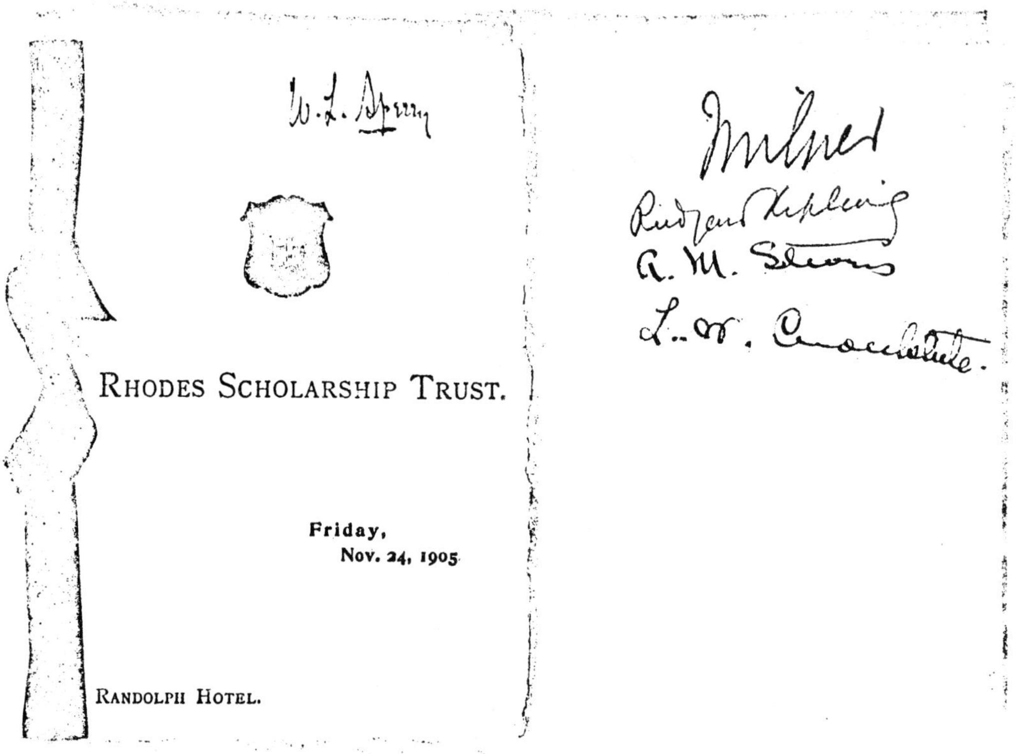

Yet, though an epoch had ended and the imperial dream was over, Rhodes's world vision had not entirely faded for Kipling. Shortly before his death in 1917, Jameson visited Bateman's to request Kipling to become one of the trustees responsible for administering the Rhodes scholarships. Kipling accepted happily. But even the Rhodes Trust was compelled to alter with the times. The old British Empire was giving way to a liberal commonwealth, and when Philip Kerr, a Liberal and internationalist (and former member of Milner's staff), was appointed Secretary of the Trust in 1925, Kipling publicly announced his resignation. This cut his last formal tie with South Africa. Only the friendships he had forged there were to last for the rest of his life.

The end of the Boer War marked the end of an epoch for Kipling himself, as well as for the Empire, but it did not reduce his output or his popularity as a writer. Almost throughout his life, he continued to be offered official honours and titles; with the exception of academic degrees, he consistently refused them. Although he would not accept the position of Poet Laureate, with its concomitant responsibilities and commitment, he did accept the highest of international honours when it was offered him. In 1907 Carrie accompanied him to Stockholm to receive the Nobel Prize for literature.

In his personal life, the early tragedy of his daughter Josephine's death was matched by the loss of his only son in 1915. Kipling had long foreseen a war with Germany; he had prophesied that the Boer War was "a first-class dress parade for

Armageddon", and had spent years in preaching the doctrine of military preparedness to an unreceptive British public. On 4 August 1914 he wrote in Carrie's diary, "Incidentally Armageddon begins."

In September their 17-year-old son John joined the Irish Guards on the nomination of their old friend, Lord Roberts. John was reported wounded and missing after the Battle of Loos, just a year later, though his death was not finally confirmed until 1917. Kipling never again wrote a lay of Empire.

Mourning for his only son found practical expression in two ways: Kipling became a member of the Imperial War Graves Commission, and he wrote a history of John's regiment, *The Irish Guards in the Great War*, published in 1923.

The strain of the war years left both Carrie and Rudyard in poor health. In 1924 their only surviving child, Elsie, married Captain George Bambridge, a former officer of the Irish Guards. Bateman's had become a gloomy place. Kipling continued to produce new work, but by the 1930s he was concentrating his efforts on putting his literary house in order. He arranged a new definitive edition of his collected verse, oversaw the preparation of the 35-volume Sussex edition of his acknow-

Opposite: Signatures from a meeting of the Rhodes Scholarship Trust in 1905 include those of two of Rhodes's closest friends, Milner and Kipling. Kipling became a trustee administering the Rhodes scholarships, which are still awarded today.

Right: Rudyard Kipling was awarded the Nobel Prize for Literature in 1907. He accepted the honour, though he had consistently refused others – including the Poet Laureateship and a knighthood.

ledged works, and began writing an enigmatic autobiography, *Something of Myself*, which he did not live to finish.

Kipling died on 18 January 1936, on the 44th anniversary of his marriage, a little more than two weeks after his 70th birthday. He and Carrie were staying at Brown's Hotel in London when he suffered a violent duodenal haemorrhage and was rushed to hospital for an emergency operation; he died five days later.

England mourned Kipling, though his death was submerged in a greater grief, coinciding as it did almost to the day with the death of the beloved monarch King George V. In a moving service in Westminster Abbey, Kipling's ashes were buried in Poet's Corner a few days before the King's funeral.

The imperialistic political views that shaped Kipling's reaction to South Africa went out of fashion, and his South African writing faded from view; it had not included any central book or even one especially outstanding story to earmark it as significant among the many works of his prodigious lifelong output.

Kipling's own interest swung away from the dream of Empire, which could not long survive Rhodes's death, and the departure of Milner and Jameson from South Africa. The touches of southern Africa that have survived undimmed are to be found in the poems and the few *Just So Stories* drawn from Kipling's travels in the sub-continent. Like certain lines in the "South Africa" chapter of his autobiography, they reveal a swift, lyrical response to landscape and light, above all else.

In keeping with this response, which was beyond politics, in his later years (as Richard Holmes has argued in his recent enlightening introduction to *Something of Myself*) Kipling was increasingly absorbed by a dream that had little to do with an earthly empire. His best loved works are radiant with a different light: already, in *Kim*, the light of memories of childhood and India, and finally, in *Puck of Pook's Hill* and *Rewards and Fairies*, the rich chiaroscuro of English history. Kipling himself spoke of these last two books as intended "to be a sort of balance to, as well as a seal upon, some aspects of my 'Imperialistic' output in the past".

The end of the South African years had spelled escape from the political hurly-burly of Empire, from the role of the public man. Moving into the second half of his life, Rudyard Kipling withdrew into an older, inner dream: the timeless world of art.

Notes

CHAPTER 1: **1** *The Star*, Johannesburg, 19 January 1936; **2** *The Kipling Journal*, April 1948, p.7; **3** "The Sin of Witchcraft", Cape Town, February 1900; **4** *The New Zealand Herald*, 27 October 1891; **5** Quoted in Charles Carrington, *Rudyard Kipling, his life and work*, p.354; **6** *Literature*, 20 May 1899.

CHAPTER 2: **1** Quoted in Lucile Russell Carpenter, *Rudyard Kipling: a friendly profile*, p.44 & 63; **2** John Hays Hammond, *The autobiography of John Hays Hammond*, p.442; **3** J G McDonald, *Rhodes: A Life*, p.393; **4** Mortimer Menpes, *War Impressions*, p.115; **5** *The African Review*, 30April 1898 **6** Letters from Olive Schreiner to Betty Molteno and William Philip Schreiner ("Laddie"), March 1898 (The Olive Schreiner Collection, University of Cape Town Libraries); **7**Quoted in Margaret Lane, *Edgar Wallace, the biography of a phenomenon, p. 100.*

CHAPTER 3: **1** *The Times*, 14 October 1899; **2** *The Kipling Journal*, December 1985, p.59; **3** Quoted in Julian Ralph, *War's Brighter Side*, p.261; **4** *The Kipling Journal*, April 1942, p.13; **5** *The Kipling Journal*, April 1942, p.13.

CHAPTER 4: **1** Quoted in Julian Ralph, *War's Brighter Side*, p.103–104; **2** Quoted *ibid*, p.258 & 132; **3** Quoted *ibid*, p.206; **4** *Ibid*, p.207; **5** *Ibid*, p.265.

CHAPTER 5: **1** Quoted in Lucile Russell Carpenter, *Rudyard Kipling: a friendly profile*, p.63; **2** *The Ladies' Home Journal*, January 1902; **3** *The National Review*, vol 114, January–June 1940; **4** Letter from Kipling to Dr James Conland, 20 February 1901 (Carpenter/Kipling Collection, Rare Book and Special Collections Division, Library of Congress); **5** Letter from Kipling to Cecil Rhodes, 14 April 1901 (The Rhodes Trust, by kind permission of the National Trust); **6** Memoir by Mrs George Bambridge, quoted in Charles Carrington, *Rudyard Kipling, his life and work*, p.511.

CHAPTER 6: **1** Quoted in Lucile Russell Carpenter, *Rudyard Kipling: a friendly profile*, p.68; **2** Letter from Kipling to Mrs Edmonia Hill, 27 June 1906 (Carpenter/Kipling Collection, Rare Book and Special Collections Division, Library of Congress); **3** Quoted in Ellis Ames Ballard, *Catalogue intimate and descriptive of my Kipling Collection*, p.246; **4** Letter from Kipling to Maitland Park, 11 July 1902 (The Kipling Collection, University of Cape Town Libraries); **5** Letter from Kipling to Herbert Baker, 4 February 1908 (Quoted by kind permission of the National Trust).

CHAPTER 7. **1** Quoted in Charles Carrington, *Rudyard Kipling, his life and work*, p.389; **2** Letter from Kipling to Charles Crewe, 17 June 1910 (Quoted by kind permission of the National Trust).

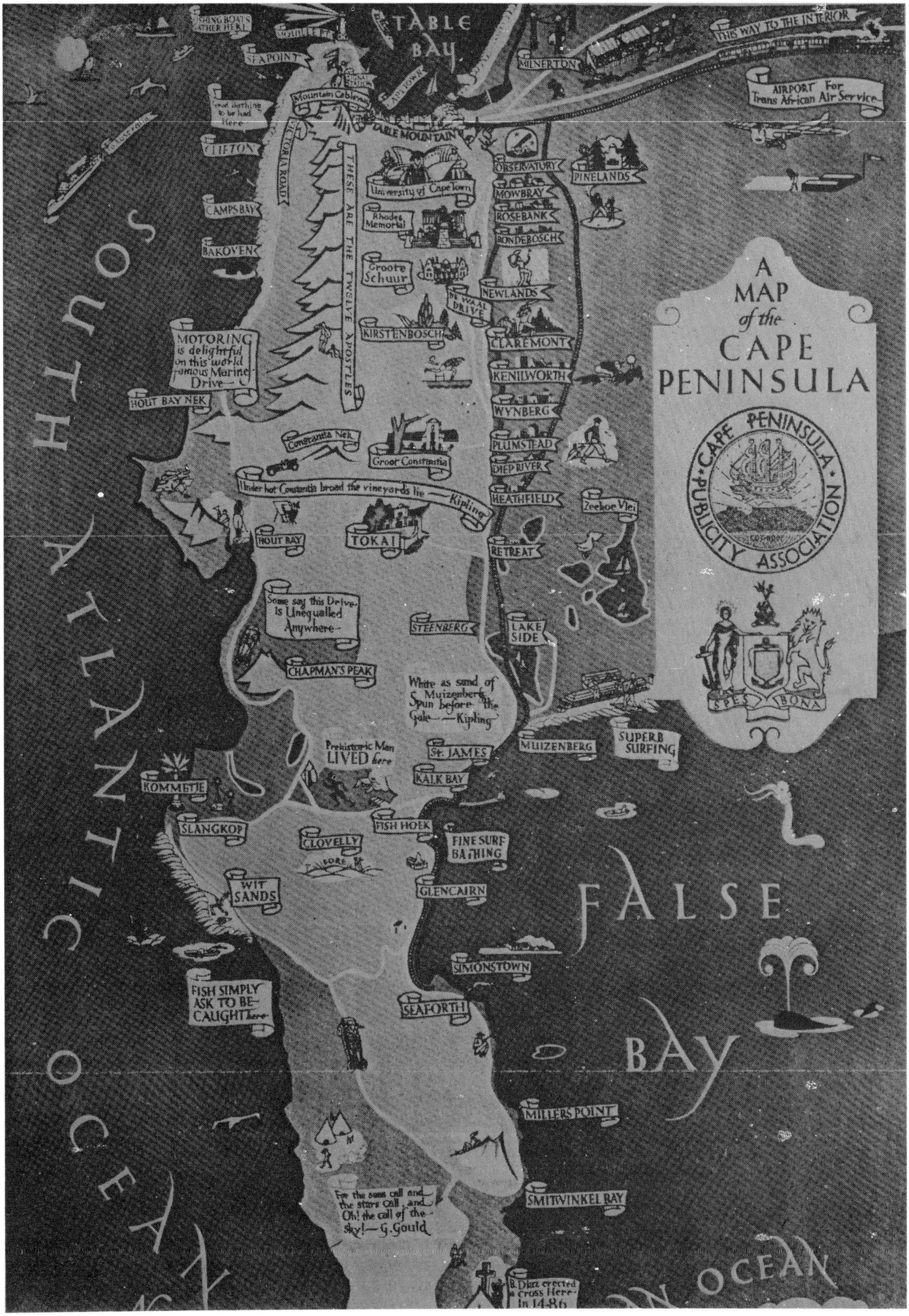

TABLE BAY
FISHING BOATS GATHER HERE
SEAPOINT
MILNERTON
THIS WAY TO THE INTERIOR
AIRPORT For Trans African Air Service
Mountain Cableway
TABLE MOUNTAIN
Good Bathing to be had Here
CLIFTON
VICTORIA ROAD
THESE ARE THE TWELVE APOSTLES
University of Cape Town
OBSERVATORY
PINELANDS
MOWBRAY
ROSEBANK
Rhodes Memorial
RONDEBOSCH
CAMPS BAY
BAKOVEN
Groote Schuur
NEWLANDS
DE WAAL DRIVE
KIRSTENBOSCH
CLAREMONT
KENILWORTH
MOTORING is delightful on this world famous Marine Drive
HOUT BAY NEK
WYNBERG
Constantia Nek
Groot Constantia
PLUMSTEAD
DIEP RIVER
Under hot Constantia broad the vineyards lie — Kipling
HEATHFIELD
Zeekoe Vlei
HOUT BAY
TOKAI
RETREAT
Some say this Drive is Unequalled Anywhere
STEENBERG
LAKE SIDE
CHAPMAN'S PEAK
White as sand of Muizenberg Spun before the Gale — Kipling
MUIZENBERG
SUPERB SURFING
Prehistoric Man LIVED here
ST. JAMES
KOMMETJIE
KALK BAY
SLANGKOP
FISH HOEK
CLOVELLY
FINE SURF BATHING
WIT SANDS
GLENCAIRN
SOUTH ATLANTIC OCEAN
FALSE BAY
SIMONSTOWN
FISH SIMPLY ASK TO BE CAUGHT here
SEAFORTH
MILLERS POINT
For the seas call and the stars call, and Oh! the call of the sky! — G. Gould
SMITWINKEL BAY
B. Diaz erected a cross Here In 1486
OCEAN
A MAP of the CAPE PENINSULA
CAPE PENINSULA PUBLICITY ASSOCIATION
SPES BONA

Picture credits

The following abbreviations have been used:
CA (Cape Archives)
KC/UCT (Kipling Collection, University of Cape Town Libraries)
OSC/UCT (Oliver Schreiner Collection, UCT Libraries)
SC/UCT) CJ Sibbett Collection, UCT Libraries)
SAL (South African Library, Cape Town)
UCT (University of Cape Town Libraries)

Frontispiece: KC/UCT

Chapter 1: **8** Queen, 1891 (UCT); **10** No E4 (CA); KC/UCT; **12** No AG 1140 (CA); **13** OSC/UCT; **14** No AG 3448 (CA); **15** & **16** Simon's Town Museum; **17** By kind permission of the National Trust, Britain; **18** SC/UCT; **19** *Star Portrait Gallery* (SAL).

Chapter 2: **21** *Rottingdeam, Story of a Village* (J Beal & Son); KC/UCT; **22** Vineyard Hotel, Cape Town; *Men of our Times* (SAL); **24** *Punch* 10 Dec 1892 (KC/UCT); **25** Greenwall Collection; **26** *African Treasures* (SAL); OSC/UCT; **27** African Review (SAL); *Owlographs;* **28** *Review of Reviews* April 1899 (KC/UCT); by kind permission of *The Kipling Journal* (organ of the Kipling Society, 18 Northumberland Ave, London WC2).

Chapter 3: **30** No E 386 (CA); **31** KC/UCT; **32** KC/UCT; **34** *War Impressions* (KC/UCT); **35** Greenwall Collection; **36** *War Impressions* (KC/UCT); Greenwall Collection; **37** Transvaal Archives; **38** Greenwall Collection; **39** Artist unknown; **40** Greenwall Collection; (cartoon) KC/UCT; **41** KC/UCT; **43** Greenwall Collection; KC/UCT; **44** Library of the University of the Witwatersrand; No AG 10602 (CA); **46** No J 4340 (CA); **47** *Strand Magazine* 24 Feb 1900, KC/UCT.

Chapter 4: **49** Creswicke (SAL); **50**, **51** & **52** *War's Brighter Side*, KC/UCT; **53** Artist unknown; Creswicke (SAL); **54** *War Impressions*, KC/UCT; **55***South Africa* 1 Sept 1900 (UCT); **56** KC/UCT; **57** *Black and White* 9 June 1900 (SAL); **59** KC/UCT; **60** *Truth* 25 Dec 1900 (KC/UCT).

Chapter 5: **62** Greenwall Collection; **63** SAL; **65** *Sketches in Mafeking and East Africa* (KC/UCT); No J 7785 (CA); **66** SC/UCT; **67** *Windsor Magazine* Oct 1901 (KC/UCT); **70** KC/UCT; **71** & **72** SC/UCT; **73** By kind permission of the Kipling Society; **74** (Woolsack) Greenwall Collection; (Baker) By kind permission of the Bank of England; *War Impressions* (KC/UCT); **75**, **76** & **77** *Truth* 25 Dec 1899 (KC/UCT); **78** *Almanac of Twelve Sports; L'Assiette au Beurre* 1 Feb 1902 (KC/UCT); **79** Greenwall Collection; **80** Private Collection; **81** *Chronical of the Funeral Ceremonies. . .* (CA).

Chapter 6: **83** *Rottingdean, Story of a Village* (J Beal & Son); **84** SAL; **86** Reprinted in *Review of Reviews* Feb 1902 (KC/UCT); **87** *War with the Boers* (SAL); **88** Simon's Town Museum; **89** SA *Merry-go-round* 9 Jan 1929 (SAL); **90** & **91** KC/UCT; **92** *Yesterday's Child* (KC/UCT); **93** SC/UCT; (Lillie Langtry) No J 12653 (CA).

Chapter 7: **94** No AG 1144 (CA); **95** Johannesburg Art Gallery; Philipp Wagner; **96** & **97** SAL; **99** *Yesterday's Child* (KC/UCT); **100**Houghton Library, Harvard University, USA; **101** *Punch* 18 Dec 1907 (SAL); and **104** Municipal reference library, Cape Town.

Chronology

1865	RK born in Bombay, India, 30 December.
1882–7	On staff of *Civil and Military Gazette*, Lahore.
1886	*Departmental Ditties* published.
1887–9	RK on staff of the *Pioneer*, Allahabad.
1888	*Plain Tales from the Hills*, and stories for the Indian Railway Library published.
1890	Literary success in London.
1891	Embarks for Cape Town in SS *Mexican* 22 August, arriving 10 September. Meets Olive Schreiner. Departs for New Zealand, Australia and India in the *Doric* 25 September.
1892	Arrives back in London 10 January. MarriesCaroline Starr Balestier 18 January. They settle in Brattleboro, Vermont, USA in July. Their first daughter, Josephine, born 29 December.
1893	"Judson and the Empire" (*Many Inventions*).
1895	Jameson Raid in South Africa (December).
1896	Rhodes resigns as Prime Minister of the Cape Colony. Kipling's second daughter, Elsie, born 2 February. Family leaves USA for England and settles in Maidencombe near Torquay.
1897	RK admitted to Athenaeum Club, dining with Sir Alfred Milner and Cecil Rhodes. Kiplings move to North End House, Rottingdean, in June. Their son, John, is born 17 August, and they move to The Elms, Rottingdean.
1898	Kipling family, with RK's father, embark from Southampton in *Dunvegan Castle* 8 January, arriving in Cape Town 25 January. Friendship with Rhodes, Milner (British High Commissioner and Governor of the Cape Colony) and Dr Jameson. RK visits Rhodes's fruit farms and travels to Rhodesia by train, exploring Bulawayo and visiting the Matopos. Returning via Johannesburg, RK is guest of honour at Rand Club dinner (2 April); meets Percy FitzPatrick. Visits Kimberley, meeting Olive Schreiner again. Kipling family depart from Cape Town in *Norham Castle* (13 April). Lengthy commentary of RK's South African visit in *African Review* 21 May.
1899	Kipling's last visit to America – Kipling family arrive in New York 2 February. RK seriously ill 20 February – 4 March. Death of eldest daughter, Josephine, 6 March. Kipling family return to their English home 24 June. RK at the height of his fame. Outbreak of Anglo-Boer War 11 October. RK forms volunteer company in the village of Rottingdean. "The Absent-minded Beggar" first published in the *Daily Mail, Pall Mall Gazette* and *New York Journal* 31 October. RK refuses knighthood. "Black Week": British defeats at Stormberg, Magersfontein and Colenso in December. Lord Roberts appointed Commander-in-Chief of British forces in South Africa.

1900 Kipling family sail for Cape in *Kinfauns Castle* 20 January, arriving 5 February to stay at Mount Nelson Hotel. RK visits military hospitals in Cape Town. Travels to Modder River railhead in ambulance train, returning with trainload of wounded mid-February.

Roberts defeats Cronje at Paardeberg; Cronje surrenders with his men.

RK elected honorary member of St George's Lodge at the Masonic Temple, Roeland Street, Cape Town. At Rhodes's invitation, Carrie accompanies architect Herbert Baker to select a site for The Woolsack 7 March.

Lord Roberts occupies Bloemfontein 13 March. Army newspaper, *The Friend*, edited by four war correspondents (Julian Ralph, Perceval Landon, H A Gwynne and F W Buxton) first appears 16 March.

"The Sin of Witchcraft" (*Uncollected*) first published in *The Times* with the title "The Exposure of Cape Population" 15 March; published in *The Friend* 10 April. RK writes "St Patrick's Day" (*Miscellaneous*) in telegraph office, Cape Town on 17 March; published in *The Friend* 17 and 23 March. Lord Roberts telegraphs RK 17 March to join *The Friend*. RK arrives in Bloemfontein to join editorial staff 21 March.

RK witnesses Battle of Karee Siding 29 March. "General Joubert" (*The Five Nations*) first published in *The Friend* 30 March (originally "The death of General Joubert"). "Fables for the staff" and "Kopje-Book Maxims" published in the *The Friend* 24 – 31 March and "A Song of the White Men" (*Miscellaneous*) on 2 April. RK returns to Cape Town 3 April.

"To the people of the Free State", appeal composed by RK and Julian Ralph, published in *The Friend* 6 April. RK writes "A new Auld Lang Syne" (*Miscellaneous*) for concert in aid of Widows' and Orphans' Fund, Bloemfontein 18 April.

Kipling family depart from Cape Town in *Tantallon Castle* 11 April, arriving in London 28 April. In Rottingdean RK launches rifle club and arranges for rifle range, drill hall and a branch of the Navy League.

"The Elephant's Child" (*Just So Stories*) first published in *The Ladies' Home Journal* in April.

"With Number Three" and "Surgical and Medical" (*Uncollected Prose II*) first published in *Daily Mail* 21 April and 1 May respectively.

"Stories of the War": "The way that he took" (*Land and Sea Tales*) first published *Daily Express* 12 June; "Folly Bridge" (*Uncollected Prose II*) *Daily Express* June and July; "The Outsider" (*Uncollected Prose II*) *Daily Express* 19 June; "A Burgher of the Free State" (*Uncollected Prose II*) *Daily Express* 26 June.

Kipling family arrives to Cape Town in *Tantallon Castle* 25 December, and moves into The Woolsack on the same day.

Kim begins appearing in *Cassell's Magazine* in January (published in book form October).

1901 RK exchanges almost daily visits with Rhodes. Rhodes Scholarships plans laid in February. RK meets Baden-Powell; renews acquaintanceship with Jameson. Proposes Maitland Park as editor of *Cape Times* (Park duly appointed 1902).

"The Science of Rebellion" (*Uncollected Prose II*) written in February (first issued as signed pamphlet in Britain).

"How the leopard got his spots" (*Just So Stories*), set on the Transvaal Highveld, first published in *Pearson's Magazine* in April.

Kipling family sail from Cape Town in the *Briton* 17 April.

Poems: "Bridge-Guard in the Karroo" (*The Five Nations*) first published in *The Times* 5 June; "The Lesson" (*The Five Nations*) in *The Times* 29 July; "M.I." (*The Five Nations*) written in September and first published in *New York Tribune* 21 September, then in *Windsor Magazine* and *McClure's Magazine* in October. "The Reformers" (*The Five Nations*) first published in *The Times* 12 October.

"A Sahib's War" (*Traffics and Discoveries*), started early in the year, first published in *The Windsor Magazine* December and *Collier's Weekly* 7 December.

Most Boer War verse written, including "Boots', "Chant-Pagan", "Columns", "Half-Ballade of Waterval", "The Instructor", "Lichtenberg", "The Married Man", "The Parting of the Columns", "Piet", "The Return", "Stellenbosch", "Two Kopjes", "Ubique", "Wilful Missing" (collected in *The Five Nations* 1903).

1902 "The Islanders" (*The Five Nations*) published in *The Times,* 4 January.

Kipling family arrive in Cape Town in *Kinfauns Castle* 7 January. RK completes "The Cat that Walked by Himself" and "The Butterfly that Stamped" (*Just So Stories*), published in *The Ladies' Home Journal* in July and October, at The Woolsack early in the year. Considers entering politics as member of the South African Progressive Party; makes a political speech at Progressive Party meeting in Metropolitan Hall, Cape Town.

Death of Rhodes 26 March.

RK and Carrie attended public ceremony in the Cathedral, Cape Town 3 April.

Formal negotiations for peace between Britain and South Africa 9 April.

"The Burial" read at Rhodes's graveside in the Matopos 10 April. Kipling family depart from Cape Town in *Walmer Castle* 16 April, with Dr Jameson and Kipling's father on board.

Treaty of Vereeniging 31 May. Peace signed in South Africa 1 June.

Kiplings purchase Bateman's at Burwash, Sussex on 10 June; move in 3 September.

"The Comprehension of Private Copper" (*Traffics and Discoveries*) first published in *The Strand* and *Everybody's Magazine* in October. "The Captive" (*Traffics and Discoveries*) first published in America as a copyright pamphlet and in *Collier's Weekly* 6 December.

Just So Stories published.

1903 Kipling family arrive in Cape Town in *Kildonan Castle 13 January.*

Poem "*The Settler*" (*The Five Nations*) first published in *The Times* 27 February.

RK and Carrie travel to Kimberley, staying with Herbert Baker, and to Pretoria, visiting Kruger's house and the Raadzaal in March.

RK joins Royal Automobile Club at Cape Town meeting 4 April. Declines to contest a Cape constituency. Kipling family sail from Cape Town in *Kinfauns Castle* 22 April, returning, after the summer at Batemans, in the *Walmer Castle* 30 December.

1904 Jameson elected Prime Minister of the Cape Colony in February.

"They" (*Traffics and Discoveries*) begun at The Woolsack in February (first published in *Scribner's Magazine* in August).

RK and Carrie visit Kimberley. Kipling family depart from Cape Town in *Kildonan Castle* 13 April.

"Mrs Bathurst" (*Traffics and Discoveries*) first published in the *Windsor Magazine* and *Metropolitan Magazine* in September.

Kipling family return to Cape Town in *Armadale Castle* 27 December.

1905 RK concerned with planning the Rhodes Memorial on Table Mountain. Much of the research for *Puck of Pook's Hill* and *Rewards and Fairies* done at the South African Public Library, Cape Town, and much of the writing at The Woolsack.

Kipling family depart from Cape Town in *Kinfauns Castle* 5 April.

Lord Milner recalled to London, resigning as Governor. RK publishes "The Pro-Consuls" (*The Years Between* and *Poems from History*), a tribute to Milner, in *The Times* 22 July.

Kipling family sail from Southampton in *Armadale Castle* 23 December.

1906 "The Silent Army": verses written and given to the Duchess of Connaught on board ship on 6 January. Kipling family arrive in Cape Town 9 January. On this visit they meet Lillie Langtry, famous English actress whose rendition of "The Absent-minded Begger" delighted 1899 audiences.

Puck of Pook's Hill published.

Kipling family depart from Cape Town in *Kinfauns Castle* 18 April.

Dingley, anti-war French novel by Jean and Jérôme Tharaud, reputedly about RK's experiences in South Africa, published and awarded the Goncourt Prize.

Kipling family sail from Southampton in *The Saxon* 14 December.

1907 Kipling family arrive in Cape Town 1 January. RK and Carrie attended unveiling ceremony of monument to Cape Town volunteers who died in Anglo-Boer War. Kipling family departs from Cape Town in *Kenilworth Castle* 3 April.

RK awarded Nobel Prize for literature in December.

1908 Last visit of the Kiplings to South Africa. They arrive in *The Saxon* 15 January.

The South African Party, led by J X Merriman, returned to power. Jameson resigns as Prime Minister of Cape Colony.

Kipling family depart from Cape Town in *Kenilworth Castle* 15 April.

1910 Union of South Africa comes into being 31 May.

Rewards and Fairies published. Poem "If" written for Dr Jameson.

1912 Unveiling of Rhodes Memorial in Cape Town 5 July, with Kipling's inscription.

1915 RK's son John reported missing, believed killed in France.

1917 Jameson dies 26 November. RK appointed one of trustees administering Rhodes Scholarship (resigns 1925).

1936 Death of RK 18 January. Ashes laid to rest in Poet's Corner, Westminister Abbey.

Select bibliography

Sir Herbert Baker, *Cecil Rhodes, by his architect, Herbert Baker* (London, 1934)
Herbert Baker and WT Stead, *Cecil Rhodes: the man and his dream* (Bulawayo, 1977)
Ellis Ames Ballard, *Catalogue intimate and descriptive of my Kipling collection, books, manuscripts and letters with reproductions of rarities, how I got them, why I prize them and what I failed to get, with inferences and opinions solely my own and probably wrong* (Philadelphia, 1935)
Lord Birkenhead, *Rudyard Kipling* (London, 1978)
Beryl Lee Booker, *Yesterday's Child, 1890–1909* (London, 1937)
Nella Braddy, *Son of Empire; the story of Rudyard Kipling* (London, 1953)
Hilton Brown, *Rudyard Kipling; a new appreciation* (London, 1945)
Lucile Russell Carpenter, *Rudyard Kipling, a friendly profile* (Chicago, 1942)
Charles Carrington, *Rudyard Kipling, his life and work* (London, 1955)
WJ Clarke, *The less familiar Kipling and Kiplingana* (London, 1917)
Morton Cohen, ed, *Rudyard Kipling to Rider Haggard: the record of a friendship* (London, 1965)
Bonamy Dobrée, *Rudyard Kipling: realist and fabulist* (London, 1967)
Roger Lancelyn Green, ed, *Reader's Guide to Rudyard Kipling's Work, prepared for* Mr R.E. *Harbord* (London, 1961–1970)
Doreen Edith Greig, *Herbert Baker in South Africa* (Cape Town, 1970)
Felix Gross, *Rhodes of Africa* (London, 1956)
Margaret Lane, *Edgar Wallace: the biography of a phenomenon* (London, 1938)
Richard Le Gallienne, *Rudyard Kipling: a criticism* (London, 1900)
Sir James Gordon McDonald, *Rhodes: A Life* (London, 1927)
VC Malherbe, *Eminent Victorians in South Africa* (Cape Town, 1972)
Ernest Walter Martindell, *A bibliography of the works of Rudyard Kipling* (London, 1922)
Mortimer Menpes, *War Impressions: being a record in colour of the South African War 1899–1902* (London, 1901)
Julian Ralph, *War's brighter side: the story of* The Friend *newspaper edited by the correspondents with Lord Roberts's forces, March–April, 1900* (London, 1901)
Gerald Shaw, *Some Beginnings: the Cape Times, 1876–1910* (Cape Town, 1975)
James McGregor Stewart, *Rudyard Kipling, a bibliographical catalogue* (Toronto, 1959)
JMS Tompkins, *The Art of Rudyard Kipling* (London, 1959)
Lady Nourah Waterhouse, *Private and official* (London, 1942)
Angus Wilson, *The Strange Ride of Rudyard Kipling: his life and works* (London, 1977)
W Arthur Young and John H McGivering, *A Kipling Dictionary* (London, 1967)

Dictionary of South African Biography (Durban and Pretoria, 1981)
Standard Encyclopaedia of Southern Africa (Cape Town and London, 1970)
The Sussex Edition of the Complete Works in Prose and Verse of Rudyard Kipling (London: Macmillan, 1938) The most definitive of the many collections of Kipling's work with his final textual revisions.

References and quotations from Kipling's writings are taken, wherever possible, from this edition
Quotations from Kipling which appear without notes are taken from his *Something of myself: for my friends known and unknown*

Index

"Absent-minded Beggar, The", 31, 32, 40, 41, 42
Afrikaner Bond, 24, 26, 66, 84, 92, 98
Allahabad, 9
Amery, LS, 42
Anglo-Boer War:
(*see also* Kipling, Rudyard: Roberts, Lord)
causes of, 29; declaration of, 30; Britain's unpreparedness, 45; "Black Week", 42; guerrilla phase, 48, 49, 53, 65, 68, 82; Treaty of Vereeniging, 82; aftermath of war, 82, 97, 99
Army and Navy, 45
"Army of a Dream", 60
Athanaeum Club, 18
Australia, 11, 15

Baden-Powell, Maj-Gen. R, 64, 91
Bailey family, 93
Bailey, (Sir) Abe, 91
Baker, (Sir) Herbert, 61, 74, 94
Baldwin family, 11
Balestier, Beatty, 16, 18
Balestier, Caroline Starr, (later Mrs Kipling), 11, 16
Balestier, Wolcott, 11, 16
Bambridge, Captain George, 101
Bambridge, Mrs George (Elsie Kipling), 70, 101
Barrack-room Ballads, 17, 26
Bateman's, 82, 83, 84, 98, 101
Bayly, Commander, 9
Beaufort West, 46
Black, Stephen, 89
"Black Week", 42
Blackwoods Magazine, 11
Bloemfontein, 48, 49, 50, 52, 53
Boer War, *See* Anglo-Boer War
Boonzaier, DC, 93
Brattleboro, 16, 17
"Bridge-Guard in the Karroo", 68, 69
British South Africa Company, 12
Bulawayo, 25
Buller, Sir Redvers, 42, 45
"Burgher of the Free State, A", 59, 89
Burleigh, Bennet, 42, 53
Burne-Jones family, 11
Burne-Jones, Lady Georgiana (Aunt Georgie), 19, 27, 82, 83
Burne-Jones, Philip, 94
Burne-Jones, Sir Edward, 27
Buxton, F W, 49

Cape Argus, 13, 89
Cape Colony, 11, 12, 13, 19, 98
Cape Times, 22, 23, 26, 91, 93
"Captive, The", 87, 89
Cassell's Magazine, 60
Chamberlain, (Sir) Joseph, 57, 75, 84
"Chant-Pagan", 86
City Club, Cape Town, 26
"City of Brass, The", 99
Civil and Military Gazette, 9, 10
Clarke, Sir Edward, 20
Colenso, battle of, 42, 45
"Comprehension of Private Copper, The", 87, 88
Conland, Dr James, 17, 21, 66, 83
Consolidated Gold Fields of South Africa, 11
"Cricket", 78
Cronjé, Commandant-General Piet, 46

Daily Express, 59
Daily Mail, 31, 41, 42, 48, 70, 82
Daily Telegraph, 42, 53
Day's Work, The, 17
De Beers Mining Company, 11
Departmental Ditties, 10
"Dirge of Dead Sisters", 85
Doubleday, Frank N, 17
Doyle, (Sir) Arthur Conan, 16
"Dykes, The", 86

"Elephant's Child, The", 70
Elms, The, 21
Express, 49

"Fables for the Staff", 51, 52
Fischer, Abraham, 98
FitzPatrick, (Sir) Percy, 25
Five Nations, The, 68, 86, 89
"Folly Bridge", 59
Fraser, Florence, 55
Friend, The, established by Lord Roberts, 49–50; RK on staff, 50–56
Friend of the Free State, 49
Fuller, Sir T E, 13

Garrett, Edmund, 22, 23
"General Joubert", 52
Gosse, Edmund, 11
Grey, Sir George, (later Earl), 94
Groote Schuur, 24, 35, 61, 64, 66, 72, 81, 92, 93, 98
Gwynne, H A, 42, 49, 50

Haggard, H Rider, 22
Hammond, John Hays, 22
Harmsworth, (Sir) Alfred, 31, 70
Helot's Dispatch, 29
"Helot's Rest", 42, 43
"How the Leopard got his Spots", 70

"If", 95
Imperial South African Association, 31, 66
Imperial War Graves Commission, 101
Irish Guards in the Great War, The, 101
"Islanders, The", 69, 75, 76–7, 86

James, Henry, 11, 16
Jameson, Dr L S ("Dr Jim"), 64, 78, 81, 82, 91, 92, 93, 95, 98, 100
Jock of the Bushveld, 26
Johannesburg, 25, 29, 42
Joubert, Commandant-General Piet, 52
"Judson and the Empire", 13
Jungle Books, The, 17, 22
Just So Stories, 70, 71, 102

Karee Siding, Battle of, 53–4
Kerr, Philip, 100
Kim, 60, 102
Kimberley, 11, 26, 42, 64
King Solomon's Mines, 22
Kingsley, Mary, 57, 85
Kipling, Alice ("Trix"), 9, 10, 27
Kipling, Caroline, (Carrie, Rudyard's wife), 16, 19, 25, 27, 28, 42, 56, 61, 66, 100, 101, 102
Kipling, Elsie, 16, 18, 21, 28, 61, 70, 72
Kipling, John, 16, 21, 28, 61, 72, 100, 101
Kipling, John Lockwood (RK's father), 16, 21, 22, 60, 82
Kipling, Josephine, 16, 21, 27, 28
Kipling, Rudyard:
(*See also* Chronology)
childhood & journalistic career, 9; literary success, 10, 11; ill health, 11; first visit to South Africa, 11 ff; marriage, 16; in America, 16–18; first summer at

the Cape, 22–27; revisits America, 27–28; ill health, death of daughter, 27, 28; atttitudes to Anglo-Boer War, 30, 31; second summer at the Cape, 42 ff; Boer war experiences, 45–48, 50–56; changing attitudes to Boer war, 57–60; Boer war stories, 59, 87–88; Boer war verse, 68–69, 85–86, 88; first summer at The Woolsack, 61–68; outcry over "The Islanders", 69, 70; *Just So Stories* completed at The Woolsack, 70; effect of death of Rhodes, 72, 81, 83; politics at the Cape, 84, 85; friendship with Maitland Park, 91–92; and with Jameson, 92, 95; involved in Rhodes Memorial, 94, 95, 96; disillusionment at outcome of Boer war, 98, 99; last summer at the Cape, 98; last ties with South Africa, 100
Kitchener, Lord, 65, 73, 82
"Kopje Book Maxims", 51
Kruger, President Paul, 29, 30, 36, 39, 52, 53, 65

Ladysmith, 42
Lahore, 9, 16
Land and Sea Tales, 59
Landon, Perceval, 42, 49, 50
Langtry, Lillie, 41, 93
Lekkerwijn, 24
"Lesson, The", 69, 86
"Lichtenberg", 56
Light that failed, The, 11
Loos, Battle of, 101

Mafeking, 42, 64
Magersfontein, 42
Maidencombe, 18, 19
"M'Andrew's Hymn", 14, 17
Many Inventions, 13
Matjiesfontein, 13
Matopos, 72
McDonald, Sir James, 24
Melbourne, 15
Menpes, Mortimer, 36, 74
Merriman, J X, 98
"M.I.", 67
Milner, Sir Alfred (later Lord), 18, 19, 23, 50, 52, 56, 64, 65, 82, 97, 98
Milner's Kindergarten, 64, 82, 97
Modder River rail-head, 46
Moore, George, 20
Mount Nelson Hotel, 42, 43, 44, 57
"Mrs Bathurst", 15
Muizenberg, 61, 71, 72, 91, 93

Nada the lily, 22
Naulahka, The, 11
Naulakha, 16, 17, 18
New York, 27, 28, 29
New Zealand, 11, 14
Newlands, Cape, 22
Nicholson, William, 78
Nobel Prize, 100, 101
North End House, 19, 20, 21, 82

"Old Issue, The", 29
Orange Free State, 29
Orange River Colony, 98
"Outsider, The", 59

Paardeberg, Battle of, 45, 46
Paarl, 24, 36
Pall Mall Magazine, 45
Park, Maitland, 91, 92, 93
"Patrol Song", 64
Phillips, Captain J, 46
"Piet", 89
Pioneer, 9, 91, 93
Plain tales from the Hills, 10
Poynter, Ambrose, 16
Poynter family, 11
Pretoria, 29, 82
"Pro-Consuls, The", 98
Progressive Party, 26, 84, 92, 98
Puck of Pook's Hill, 98, 102
Punch, 58

Ralph, Julian, 42, 49, 50, 54, 56
Rand Club, 25
"Recessional", 20, 58
Reuters, 42
Rewards and Fairies, 98, 102
Rhodes, Cecil John, 11, 12, 18, 19, 24, 26, 35, 36, 40, 42; friendship with RK in South Africa, 23, 64; offers The Woolsack to RK, 61; failing health, 65, 72; scholarship scheme, 65, 66; death, 72; funeral, 72, 81, 83
Rhodes, Frank, 81
Rhodes Memorial, 74, 94, 95, 96
Rhodes Scholarship Trust, 100, 101
Rhodesia, 25, 70, 72
Robinson, E Kay, 9, 17
Roberts, Freddy, 44, 45
Roberts, Lord, 17, 39, 44, 101; appointed Commander-in-Chief in South Africa, 45; defeats Cronjé at Paardeberg, 46; occupies Bloemfontein, 49; establishes *The Friend*, 49, 50
Rondebosch, 24, 45, 47
Rottingdean, 19, 21, 28, 57, 82

Royal Automobile Club, Cape Town, 91

"Sahib's War, A", 54, 87, 88
Schreiner, Olive, 13, 26
Scully, W C, 44
"Science of Rebellion, The", 66
"Service Man, The", 85, 86
"Service Songs", 85, 86, 89
"Settler, The", 85, 88
Seven Seas, The, 14, 17
Simon's Town, 9, 13, 15, 16, 26, 57, 89
"Sin of Witchcraft, The", 57, 66
Something of Myself, 45, 102
"Song of the Wise Children", 23
South Africa Act (1910), 99
South Africa Bill (1909), 98
South African Party, 26, 98
South African Library, 98
Spectator, The, 59
Stanley, Lord, 49
Star, The, 49
"Stories of the War", 59, 87
Stormberg, 42
Story of an African farm, 13
Struben family, 83
Sullivan, Sir Arthur, 41, 42
"Surgical and Medical", 45
Swan, J M, 94

Times, The, 18, 20, 29, 42, 66, 68, 69, 85, 88
Traffics and Discoveries, 15, 87
Transvaal, 29, 30, 31, 68, 70, 88, 98
Treaty of Vereeniging, 82
Tree, Lady, 41
Trotter, Mrs, 22
Truth, 43, 75

Uitlanders, 25, 29, 88
Union Castle Line, 12, 91
Union of South Africa, 99
Union Steamship Company, 13

Vanity Fair, 17, 35, 78
"Verzoeningslied", 85
Vineyard Hotel, 22

Wallace, Edgar, 26, 27, 70, 82
Watt, A P, 11
Watts, G F, 94, 95
"Way that he Took, The", 59
"With Number Three", 48, 68
Witwatersrand, 11
Woodville, R Caton, 31, 41
Woolsack, The, 61, 62, 64, 66, 68, 72, 74, 81, 91, 98
Wynberg, 45